Smart in the Middle Grades:
Classrooms That Work for Bright Middle Schoolers

Smart in the Middle Grades:
Classrooms That Work for Bright Middle Schoolers

Carol Ann Tomlinson

Kristina Doubet

National Middle School Association
Westerville, Ohio

National Middle School Association
4151 Executive Parkway, Suite 300
Westerville, Ohio 43081
NMSA® www.nmsa.org

Sue Swaim, Executive Director
Jeff Ward, Deputy Executive Director
Edward Brazee, Editor, Professional Publications
John Lounsbury, Consulting Editor, Professional Publications
April Tibbles, Director of Publications
Mary Mitchell, Designer, Editorial Assistant
Dawn Williams, Publications Manager
Mark Shumaker, Graphic Designer
Lindsay Brown, Graphic Desinger
Cheri Howman, Copy Editor/Proofreader
Marcia Meade-Hurst, Senior Publications Representative

ISBN 10: 1-56090-195-0
ISBN 13: 978-1-56090-195-2

Library of Congress Cataloging-in-Publication Data
Tomlinson, Carol A.
  Smart in the middle grades: classrooms that work for bright middle
  schoolers/Carol Ann Tomlinson, Kristina Doubet.
      p. cm
  Includes bibliographical references.
  ISBN-13: 978-1-5600900195-2 (pbk.)
  ISBN-10: 1-56090-195-0
    1. Gifted children--Education (Middle school)--United states. 2. Middle
  school teaching--United states. I. Doubet, Kristina, date-II. Title.

LC3993.23.T66 2006
371.95'73--dc22   2006047342

For all the kids at Warrenton Junior High

and Warrenton Middle School

Who aren't kids any more

Except in our memories.

Thanks for those memories that

Go with us everywhere

Every day.

Contents

About the Authors

Carol Ann Tomlinson is professor of educational leadership, foundations, and policy at the University of Virginia's Curry School of Education. This former middle school teacher of 20 years was Virginia's Teacher of the Year in 1974. Since joining the faculty at the University of Virginia, she has authored or co-authored more than 15 books on differentiated instruction and curriculum including *How to Differentiate Instruction in Mixed-Ability Classrooms, Fulfilling the Promise of the Differentiated Classroom: Strategies and Tools for Responsive Teaching,* and *The Parallel Curriculum Model: A Design to Develop High Potential and Challenge High Ability Learners.* Carol's work has been so well received that she travels across the U.S. and abroad to work with educators who want to develop classrooms that are more responsive to academically diverse students. She is also co-director of the university's Institutes on Academic Diversity.

Kristina Doubet is assistant professor of middle, secondary, and mathematics education at James Madison University's College of Education in Harrisonburg, Virginia. After 10 years of teaching English—9 at the middle school level—she completed her graduate work at the University of Virginia, where she earned M.Ed. and Ph.D. degrees in curriculum and instruction with an emphasis in gifted education. While there, she served as an instructor to preservice teachers and worked with a talent development program at a local middle school to develop high-quality, challenging curriculum for traditionally underserved, low-income and minority populations. She now works with practicing teachers—both nationally and abroad—as a staff developer and faculty coach for schools and districts implementing differentiated instruction.

Foreword

*Excellent teachers of young adolescents are shepherds of
possibility, helping students articulate, envision, and chart
a course to the future.* —Tomlinson & Doubet, 2006

In *Smart in the Middle Grades: Classrooms That Work for Bright
Middle Schoolers,* authors Carol Ann Tomlinson and Kristina Doubet
assert, "We believe that the needs of bright kids can be proactively,
effectively, and wisely met in the context of the middle school concept."
These veteran educators then demonstrate clearly how to implement that
vision. This book provides a much-needed and sound new resource for
educators actively engaged in educating young adolescents, especially
students with high ability and high potential. The research-based and
classroom-tested strategies described in this publication address the
special needs of our brightest students as well as other middle level
students.

Over the years, middle level and gifted educators have recognized
that the two fields are not only compatible but quite parallel, and that
practices recommended in both areas are comparable and help fulfill our
common commitment to a quality education for every young adolescent.
Recognizing this, National Association for Gifted Children (NAGC) and
National Middle School Association (NMSA) developed a joint position
statement that focuses on our common beliefs and calls for collaborative
action.

To successfully educate our nation's 20 million 10- to 15-year-old
students, everyone associated with middle level schools must understand
the full range of the cognitive and affective needs of naturally diverse
middle level students. Our joint position statement acknowledges that the
variance in middle level students requires those who serve them to be
fully aware of their diversity and to possess the skills necessary to address
the full range of learners—including those who have already demonstrated
advanced academic abilities and those who have potential that has not

yet surfaced. The joint statement highlights the commitment of National Middle School Association and National Association for Gifted Children to ensure that all middle school students learn in classrooms where equity and excellence are continuing goals for every learner.

The 2005 NAGC *State of the States Report* provided answers to the query, "What are the top three delivery methods through which gifted services are provided in the middle school?" More than two-thirds of all respondents indicated the regular classroom. While troubling to advocates of gifted education, this telling response emphasizes how important it is that classroom teachers, who often have no training in gifted education, receive guidance and support in engaging and stimulating high ability students.

A fundamental education goal is the continued intellectual growth of all students. Students whose abilities have been recognized need to be challenged to work to even higher levels, acquire new knowledge, and gain in-depth understandings. And those students whose potential has not yet been tapped especially need educational experiences that will draw out their dormant abilities. The intellectual capacities of all students need to be developed fully, not only to prepare them for the academic rigors of high school, but for a full and productive life.

We are excited about the release of this new resource by these two lifelong advocates for young adolescents. We encourage all middle level educators to read it thoughtfully and start implementing these strategies in their schools and classrooms. *Smart in the Middle Grades: Classrooms That Work for Bright Middle Schoolers* demonstrates how the shared vision found in NAGC and NMSA's joint position statement can expand learning for all our students in positive ways. Veteran middle level teachers, as well as those new to teaching in middle schools will appreciate the clear descriptions of bright middle grades students and the rationale for why we must recognize their special abilities and qualities. The chapters of this book are full to overflowing with specifics about teaching young adolescents—particularly, but not exclusively, high ability and high potential students.

With chapters on the role of the learning environment and the role of curriculum in developing and extending ability, the stage is set for an in-depth discussion of extending the challenge of quality curriculum. One chapter identifies seven instructional strategies—*Compacting, Problem-Based Learning, Complex Instruction,* and more—followed by a narrative chapter that describes those strategies and principles at work in responsive middle grades classrooms. The final chapter brings the book full circle with a series of frequently asked questions. Without a doubt, this is a book any middle level teacher who is committed to helping students grow intellectually will find indispensable.

Building the middle school culture that supports educational excellence for all students requires a long-term commitment to cooperation and growth. National Association for Gifted Children and National Middle School Association will continue our efforts to raise awareness about the diverse needs of advanced students and to seek out quality resources, such as *Smart in the Middle Grades.* We encourage school leaders and middle level practitioners to capitalize on this new, practical resource and develop the expertise that will support effective middle level teaching, particularly for high ability and high potential learners.

Sue Swaim
Executive Director
National Middle School Association

Nancy Green
Executive Director
National Association
for Gifted Children

Introduction

Bright Kids in the Middle Grades: What's the Big Deal Anyhow?

B right kids are a part of every school population—certainly including the middle grades population. That's not exactly a revelation. So why devote a book to the topic of teaching bright students in middle school?

1. As educators we constantly need to enhance our understanding of the various sorts of students we teach—whether they have learning disabilities, are struggling to read, have difficulty controlling their attention or emotions, come from cultures other than the predominate culture of the school, are highly creative, or are cognitively advanced for their age. Knowing more about the full range of our students prepares us to address their unique and common needs.

2. A book on teaching highly able learners in the middle grades is worthwhile because we often, mistakenly, look at bright kids as the ones who don't really need us—the ones who are going to be okay anyhow. In our push to help struggling kids stay afloat academically, we look gratefully at the student who is doing well in class—and turn our backs to the many students who we perceive "need us." In fact, all students need teachers to help them become the best they can be. If we truly believe some able students don't need or merit our attention, we should perhaps post a sign on the classroom door that says, "Sorry, no plans here to ensure the growth of smart kids!" While few of us overtly intend to shortchange very bright students, it is a remarkably common outcome in classes where so many students have so many needs. We hope that guidance on challenging advanced

learners in the context of other learners whose needs are great will reduce the need for posting a sign that says, "Bright kids are on their own in this classroom!"

3. A book on teaching highly able kids in the middle grades should help middle grades educators rethink the concept of what a bright kid "looks like." Certainly, there are students whose abilities overtly dazzle us. They absolutely call us to extend our reach as teachers. However, there are also many middle grades students whose advanced ability or potential is disguised by learning disabilities, poverty, emotional problems, anger or alienation, issues related to culture or race, and a score of other "masks" that can cause teachers to miss evidence of great potential. The middle school concept is rooted in the belief that early adolescence may be the last opportunity to help many students develop a sense of self-worth, competence, and self-efficacy. To that end, it is important to revisit what "smart" looks like and to consider how middle level educators can give more students the chance to be smart.

4. Much of what it takes to develop the capacities of highly able learners benefits virtually all students. That statement does not mean that as long as we "teach well," bright students will be appropriately challenged. There are definitely particular kinds of extension and support that are necessary catalysts for growth in advanced learners. Nonetheless, the *underpinnings* of quality curriculum and instruction for bright kids are also the underpinnings of quality education for all other students. Therefore, as we lay the foundations for challenging our most advanced learners, we improve the prospect for all our students.

In the end, it's important to us to write this book because both of us are simultaneously champions of the middle school concept and of bright kids. Combined, we have spent more than 30 years teaching young adolescents. We believe in the ideals of the middle school concept. We also believe the middle grades are pivotal in the development of very bright learners—as it is in the development of other students. In the past, there have been tensions between champions of middle schools and champions of the education of highly able learners. The authors of this book believe—as do many advocates of middle school education and gifted education—that the goals of the two fields are compatible and that both practices are stronger when advocates join in a search for common ground than when they expend efforts in more oppositional pursuits. The authors of this book—like many educators—are dreamers. We believe that the needs of bright kids can be proactively, effectively, and wisely met within the context of the middle school concept. We want to share that vision with others who believe likewise or are willing to consider becoming believers. We hope you are one of them.

> *We believe that the needs of bright kids can be proactively, effectively, and wisely met within the context of the middle school concept.*

What's In Store For You Here?

Our intent for the book is twofold: first, to draw on the best research available about effective teaching in general and effective teaching of high ability and high potential learners in particular; and second, to present practical ideas rooted in that research in a way that is accessible to middle grades practitioners. In other words, we want what we share to be defensible and useful.

Chapter One examines what we know about who we teach—the nature of early adolescence in general and the unique needs of highly able young adolescents in particular. The chapter includes a look at "twice exceptional" middle schoolers—those who have both high ability or high potential and a simultaneous barrier to learning, such as a learning disability, poverty, or literacy issues.

Chapter Two underscores the importance of developing positive classroom learning environments to address the needs of young adolescents, in particular, high potential and high ability young adolescents. The chapter examines affective needs shared by virtually all young adolescents and particular affective needs of highly able middle schoolers, noting the importance of learning environment in addressing those needs.

Chapter Three explores what we should teach in the middle grades—or the nature of effective middle grades curriculum. The chapter examines the characteristics of quality curriculum that span grade levels, particular goals of curriculum in the middle school, and the attributes of curriculum that provide appropriate challenge for middle schoolers with high potential or high performance.

Chapter Four looks at what it means (and what it does *not* mean) to challenge highly able learners—even beyond the challenge provided by quality curriculum. It capsules several models for thinking about and planning high-end challenge and spells out principles that can guide teachers as they plan for high ability and high potential learners.

Chapter Five unpacks a few specific instructional strategies that, when used appropriately, can help middle school teachers challenge bright and talented kids. Because we believe that most instructional strategies are useful for most students, the chapter explains the strategies and notes ways in which they may be adapted to meet varied learner needs— including those of high potential and high-performing young adolescents.

Chapter Six presents classroom scenarios that depict how the principles and strategies discussed in earlier chapters might look when they are put to work in middle grades classrooms.

Chapter Seven addresses some frequently asked questions about teaching high ability and high potential learners in the middle grades.

Each chapter ends with a brief list of resources for learning more about the chapter topic.

A Word About Vocabulary

Words matter. They can open us up to new ways of thinking—or shut us down. They can clarify meaning—or cloud it. With the hope of encouraging new ways of thinking and clarifying meaning, we'd like to say a bit about a vocabulary decision we've made for this book.

The usual term used to designate high ability learners is "gifted." It's a word with a long history and one that serves a variety of purposes. For the most part, however, we are not going to use that term. Instead, you'll find us using words like "smart," "bright," "advanced," "high ability," "high performance," and "high potential."

Neither of us objects to the term "gifted"; and, in fact, we use it regularly in our work. Nonetheless, we've opted for synonyms for several reasons. First, the word "gifted" carries a certain amount of baggage for some educators. Right or wrong, it can connote privilege, exclusivity, and entitlement. We find value in trying to leave the baggage on the sidelines to the degree that it's possible.

> *The word "gifted" carries a certain amount of baggage for some educators.*

Second, the term "gifted" sometimes suggests formal school identification. To a degree, that's true; it's easy for educators to draw the conclusion that there is a specific and finite group of students who need additional challenge in school. While it is the case that students identified as gifted typically do need additional challenge beyond the standard curriculum, it is also the case that there are many students never identified as eligible for any special program who would benefit immensely if we saw them as highly able and responded accordingly. In this book, we want to cast a wide net in thinking about middle grades students whom educators should regard as "smart" and in need of particular challenge and support. For that reason also, we've elected to use several terms that are more inclusive.

Whatever the terms we use, we are referring to a diverse group of learners. We are talking about kids who are clearly advanced in math, science, English, social studies, foreign language, art, music, and so on. And we are talking about kids who excel with computers, in leadership, design, and other areas that have, or could have, a direct bearing on their academic success. We're talking about kids who excel and whose school agenda revolves around getting right answers; and we're talking about kids who excel in more "divergent" or "original" types of thinking.

We are talking about students who consistently perform well beyond grade level in one subject—or many. We are also talking about middle schoolers who *could* perform at consistently advanced levels, but who sometimes (or often) do not. These inconsistent performers give us glimpses of their capacity, but have not found academic achievement to be a way of life.

We are also talking about students who rarely "look" advanced. They may come from low-income backgrounds, be learning English for the first time, struggle with emotions, have a learning disability or some other handicap, or overtly reject school. Yet when we look closely at them, there are clues we shouldn't miss.

There's David—a student with a learning disability who has difficulty completing assignments and taking tests under time constraints but creates insightful products when he can select a mode of expression other than writing. There's Cody, a student from a low-income home whose standardized test scores are barely in the top quartile, but if we compare his scores to those of many of his neighborhood peers—rather than to those of more privileged peers—they look pretty impressive. There's Misha who has trouble understanding the language of the classroom, but who faithfully makes lists of words from class and television and who comes quietly to the teacher to ask questions. There's Erika who makes good grades then makes sure her friends don't know about them.

All of these students are "bright" or "smart." Some of them are high-performing, while others have high potential but have not yet "grown into it" or become comfortable with that potential.

This book is about teaching both the blatantly bright middle schooler *and* the "closet" smart kid. We believe that the most powerful teaching happens when a teacher envisions each student's very best and creates a classroom in which each student can discover his or her own personal best and work, with adult and peer support, to achieve it.

> *The most powerful teaching happens when a teacher envisions each student's very best and creates a classroom in which each student can discover his or her own personal best and work, with adult and peer support, to achieve it.*

We appreciate your interest in thinking along with us and hope you'll find the book helpful in understanding the needs of high-performing and high potential middle schoolers and in expanding your repertoire of strategies for teaching this diverse group of middle level learners. ❖

1

Being a Middle Schooler —and Smart

I need you to know that ... I'm a complicated kid—I'm shy, outgoing and standoffish, the most sarcastic person you've ever met, brutally honest, stubborn, and obnoxious. I am a leader, but I sometimes have to let others take the reins when I give up. I have zero confidence, yet I don't care what others think. I'm too ironic for my own good. I don't understand why my intelligence puts people off. I love melodrama, but petty drama is the most annoying thing. I secretly envy people, I hate myself, I love myself. ... I want to learn how to empower other people and myself.

—Lexie, 8th Grade

There is no "standard issue" young adolescent. Each one develops according to his or her own timetable and in response to his or her own unique biological makeup, environment, and opportunity. Nonetheless, the developmental period we call "early adolescence" sets broad parameters within which individual variance occurs.

Young adolescents often have big dreams—and short attention spans. They are 4 feet two inches and 5 feet 10 inches tall or more. They are consumed with self but have a compulsion to change the world. They are children becoming adults, and the transformation creates havoc in their bodies, minds, and hearts as well as in the lives of the adults who care about them. No other period in life besides infancy is so typified by physical, emotional, and intellectual change as is early adolescence.

Middle schoolers are more often carried along by the waves of change than they are directors of the change. Almost moment by moment, they wonder at the transformation and ask, "Who am I?" "What's happening to me?" "How do I fit?" and "Where do I belong?" They seem sometimes to languish as they stare into deep pools of self-absorption—into both literal and figurative mirrors. Parents and teachers could justly conclude, "Ah, I get it. Narcissus must have been a middle schooler!"

The Physiology of It All

It's not unusual for middle grades teachers to survey their students with wonder after an extended winter break because of the marked physical changes that have occurred in such a short time. Young teens' bodies often transform rapidly, producing several "side effects" with which both teachers and students must contend in the classroom.

1. Movement is necessary. Student requests to go the restroom, pencil sharpener, or trash can indicate both a need to move and an abbreviated attention span—as do tapping on desks and fidgeting in seats. Effective teachers of young adolescents understand the need for frequent "gear shifts" during a single class and plan accordingly.

2. Awkwardness is inevitable. Young adolescents' limbs grow in length first, then their bodies increase in breadth. Their trunks don't catch up with the other growth for about a year. Only then does muscular strength mature. Grace and agility are not hallmarks of early adolescence. While the pattern of development is generally consistent, it takes place on very different timetables for different students, with girls generally reaching their mature height about two years before their male peers. Effective teachers of young adolescents take into account both the awkward patterns of physical development and its variations among students.

3. A new influx of hormones contributes to both physical and social-emotional disarray. The hormone-driven changes occur at different times for different students—a reality that can itself be disorienting for middle schoolers. For some, the opposite sex becomes a prevalent

source of interest, attention, and concern. For others, the sudden preoccupation of their friends is puzzling, if not alienating. Good teachers of middle schoolers work around, rather than against, the influx of hormones. That is, they both plan for productive student interactions and simultaneously work to help students focus on important tasks at hand.

4. The young adolescent brain is in a promising state of flux. Again, this signals the most transformational developmental period other than infancy. New synapses are developing at a rapid pace, and we now understand that early adolescence is a "use-it-or-lose-it" time for the brain. The newly developing synapses are fragile and require considerable practice and support for maximum development. Synapses exercised during this period will continue development, and those not exercised will be "pruned" or lost; therefore, teachers of young adolescents should persistently call on students to reason, think abstractly, and exercise critical analysis—and provide consistent support systems for students learning how to do so.

5. Tasks or events requiring organization, planning, and reflective decision making are particularly problematic for middle schoolers. The prefrontal cortex—the part of the brain responsible for these functions—is the last portion of the brain to mature during adolescence; however, the amygdala—the emotional or "gut reaction" center of the brain—operates at full capacity. Thus, disorganization and impulsivity frequently "come with the package" of the young adolescent. Young teens can develop organizational skills but will need the watchful assistance and coaching of adults to do so. Effective teachers of 10- to 15-year-olds anticipate the challenges of organization, planning, and reflective decision making and actively play the roles of coach and guide for their students in these areas.

6. Young adolescents often feel both pulled toward and repelled by the adults in their lives. A key developmental task of teens is establishing independence. That task is both alluring and terrifying to young teens who may on one day long for the security of childhood and on the next yearn to lurch toward adulthood. This contradiction

can be as confusing for the adults who want to guide students in this developmental period as it is for the young people themselves. Excellent teachers of middle schoolers understand the ambivalence of their students toward adults. They provide environments that allow both safety and independence; they remain constant in their support of their students, even when students resist them, and they do not take personally a student's need to separate from adult authority.

7. Emotions rule. Because the portions of the brain responsible for reasoning and logic are still developing during the early adolescent years, the emotional center of the brain, which is more fully developed, often reigns supreme. Egocentrism is often a driving force for the young teen. What others think is typically of great concern. In this time span, adolescents often feel they are "on stage"—an object of scrutiny by everyone. They are sensitive to criticism—a state magnified by rapid body changes and rapid role shifts. They feel vulnerable and uncertain. "Fitting in" with peers can become paramount as middle schoolers seek a place to belong. Uniqueness and individuality often take a back seat to conformity, and middle schoolers can become quite intolerant of and cruel to students who don't fit the mold. Effective teachers understand the conflicts their students face and are willing to walk the tightrope of offering important structure and guidance while, at the same time, providing opportunities for self-exploration, independent decision making, and the development of social responsiblity.

> *The best teachers of young adolescents are shepherds of possibility—helping students articulate, envision, and chart a course to the future.*

It is the dynamic of these young adolescent markers that makes the middle school classroom at once energizing and confounding for teachers and students alike. Students at this age are driven by an urge to become something grander than their dreams, despite the lack of maturity to fully do so. The best teachers of young adolescents at this age are shepherds of possibility—helping students articulate, envision, and chart a course to the future.

Middle grades students who demonstrate advanced academic performance or who have advanced academic potential are still young adolescents. They experience the developmental stages, challenges, and needs of their contemporaries. To understand something about the hallmarks of young adolescents in general is a great first step in understanding something about highly able middle schoolers as well.

Bright middle level learners also need teachers who provide understanding, safety, challenge, guidance, structure, opportunities for growing independence, scaffolding to extend their reach, a vision of what's possible, and tools for the journey toward a productive adulthood. Their advanced abilities can add an additional "ingredient" of complexity to the young adolescent cauldron of uncertainty. A teacher who plays a key role in the lives of bright middle schoolers needs to understand both general challenges these students face because of their developmental stage and specific challenges that may result from being a high-performing or high potential learner.

A good way to understand some of the by-products of being both a young adolescent and a high capability learner is to meet a few such students and to look briefly inside their minds as they experience school.

Meet Some High Ability Middle School Students

Noah is very small—the smallest student in his seventh-grade class, by far. In social studies and other classes he fidgets all the time, drumming on the desk, jiggling his legs as he reads or listens to the teacher. He giggles a lot, often at things that don't seem particularly funny to anyone else. He is prone to blurt out comments at inopportune times. The social studies teacher told his mom Noah was immature, but that he would grow out of it. In reality, Noah's intellectual development has outstripped his physical and social development. He knows a great deal about history and finds the pace of class very tedious. He'd like to offer comments about topics the class is studying, but when he does, the teacher seems to find them off the mark. His giggling is because he sees irony, paradox, and humor in what seems merely factual to many other students. At the same time, Noah is very sensitive about his size. The other kids often treat him like a child, and while he doesn't like that, he doesn't know what to do about it. These days, he's feeling like it's safer to lay low, be quiet, keep to himself—but he'd love to have some friends, especially some friends who like history.

Heather appears very mature for her age. Heather's work always exceeds the teacher's expectations and often gives insight to the teacher. Heather follows instructions wonderfully, provides a sort of quiet leadership for the students around her, and often offers to help the teacher with various chores. Her English teacher sometimes wishes she could clone Heather to have a student like her in every class. While Heather doesn't seem to be wildly popular (the teacher thinks that's because she's too mature for the other students), the kids respect her. This is a kid the teacher can trust to be on autopilot—one who doesn't require much "maintenance" from the teacher. If Heather could talk honestly with the teacher—which she wouldn't dare do—she'd tell her several things. She'd tell her that she feels left out and ignored because the teacher doesn't tease her like she does many of the other kids. To Heather, the teasing is a sign of acceptance, and she wishes she understood why the teacher doesn't like her. She'd tell the teacher she wishes she knew how to become a better writer. The teacher gives her As on everything she writes, but Heather knows she's not growing, and so she feels like the As are dishonest to some degree. Heather would also tell her teacher that she enjoys spending time with her because the teacher is a better conversationalist than her peers, and she sometimes gets hungry for good conversations.

"**Elijah** has retreated into himself again," Mr. Ortega observes with dismay. Elijah's grades hover in the mid-C range, and he rarely contributes to class discussions, despite being a "natural" with science and having a curiosity about the world around him. His teacher gets discouraged when, time after time, he sees Elijah on the verge of academic success, only to watch his effort plummet again. Elijah was a better student at the beginning of the year than he is as the class moves toward midterm of second semester. If Elijah dared talk with Mr. Ortega, he'd tell him he likes science a lot and even reads extra about it at home. He'd tell his teacher that he's tired of his peers teasing him for doing homework—tired of them calling him "white" because he cares about grades. He'd tell Mr. Ortega not to give up on him but not to call attention to him in class either. He wants to be a good student, but he can't pull away from his friends. It's making him angry to feel pulled in both directions at once. His parents push him to do well in school, and that's beginning to make him mad. They don't understand him.

Julia did great in elementary school. Creativity was her hallmark—her saving grace. Whatever project was assigned, Julia did it with a flourish. "You can count on her to come at assignments in a fresh way," a teacher once wrote on her report card. Because of her elementary school success, Julia was assigned to several advanced classes in middle school, where she now feels like she is sinking all the time. Several of her teachers feel she is misplaced—that she isn't an advanced student at all. The teachers give acres of notes. Homework is practicing facts and skills. Tests are about single—and to Julia, mysterious—right answers. Nothing seems to make sense to her, and there is no opportunity to think about things divergently or to come at things in a different way. She has come to hate middle school, and she'd tell her teachers that, if they'd give her a chance. Her friends used to like her because she was different; now they seem to reject her for the very same reason. She learned a lot when she could think about topics broadly and divergently. Now she isn't learning much of anything. Asking unexpected questions is what makes the subject matter come alive for her. She isn't studying any less at home than she ever has. In fact, she is spending more time on schoolwork, but she just can't seem to learn in that memorize-the-facts-and-give-them-back kind of way. She doesn't know how to learn in ways the teachers expect now. And she doesn't know how to be like everyone else so that her peers will like her.

Ray is a sort of middle school Pigpen. Everything he touches seems to unravel. His backpack is a disaster area. His locker is so jammed that it won't open. He regularly loses homework papers that he swears he's completed. His handwriting is illegible. Logic is seldom evident in his writing. His peers don't seem to dislike him as a person, but they don't want him in a working group because he somehow seems to "mess up everything" without any intent to do so. Yet sometimes in class discussions, he makes an observation that rivets both the teacher and his peers with its depth. One day he saw the looks of amazement on everyone's face when he offered an interpretation. "I know," he said, "sometimes I amaze myself, too." Ray's grades are abysmal because he doesn't follow directions, has so many missing homework assignments, is so random in his approach to writing, and turns in such slovenly papers. And yet, there is clearly something important going on in his mind. He said once that he wished he felt like one person instead of two, and that he didn't really care to be a geek—he just wanted to be a regular kid.

Domenic waits out math class. He received support services for English Language Learners (ELL) in much of elementary school, but he has always been fascinated by numbers. He likes their constancy, maneuverability, and especially their utility. In fifth grade, he began helping his parents with their family business on weekends and after school. He liked helping his father with inventory, the books—anything that allowed him to use math. Despite his practical ability with math, and perhaps because of his ELL label, Domenic remained in low math groups throughout elementary school. His discomfort with English and the reticence that stemmed from his cultural background made it impossible for him to speak up and assert himself. His parents believed his teachers would do what was right for him, and so they never questioned class or group placements. In middle school, he continues with less challenging math. It is boring, but he doesn't care anymore. He is good with the real math—the stuff people need to do to get a job—so he continues to fly under the radar at school.

Jasmine has just completed the objective portion of her science test. She'll get some of the answers right, but she's afraid the essay portions of the test will be different. She has a learning disability that causes her great difficulty with spelling and writing. She wrote to her science teacher on the first day of class, "My riting may make me lok stupid, but I jist get the leters mixed up. I love books and I love to read, but my head gets clowded wen I half to take a test. It doesnt mean I don't understand becauz I do. The letters swim on the paper and I panik." It takes Jasmine longer than her peers to read a chapter or take a test. She has difficulty with multiple choice questions and even more difficulty composing paragraphs or essays; yet her understanding of content runs much deeper than that of most of her peers. She hates feeling and looking stupid and knowing kids in the class think she's stupid. She feels like she's smart, but her teachers don't treat her that way, and her grades suggest her teachers are correct. She wishes there were room in school to spend time on what she *can* do rather than only on what she *can't* do.

Lavon went to six different elementary schools in five states. He has never had a real home to live in; he and his mom and his brother have moved around, staying with relatives, living in shelters. Lavon has a killer smile. Kids like him, but he has no friends; he's never been anywhere long enough to make any. It looks like he'll be in the same school for all of sixth grade, however, and he's glad. He's tired of moving. He wants to be part of something. He'd like to be a good student, but he doesn't know how. He's behind in everything. It doesn't matter much anyhow, because he'll get a job as soon as he can get out of school. Nobody in his family has ever attended college. There's no money for college, not even for a crummy apartment. Still, he had a couple of teachers along the way who made learning good. He'd like to feel that again.

Charlie loves it when the teacher makes it absolutely clear how papers will be graded. He wants to make sure he knows the game plan, and then he will invest whatever time it takes to get his work like the teacher wants it. Using that trusty approach to school success, Charlie has always been a straight A student. Now in middle school, however, he has two teachers who push him to think critically, to propose questions for inquiry, to develop innovative ways of demonstrating what he is learning. Charlie's mother spends a good deal of time at school or on the phone with those two teachers. The assignments, she says, are not fair. The teachers are expecting too much of seventh graders, or their grading criteria are not clear, or they are giving him harder work than they give other students. Charlie is frustrated. He's always been the smartest kid in the class. If he's not that smart anymore, his parents will be disappointed. If he's not a smart kid, who is he? He doesn't know how to do what the teachers want any more, but it's got to be the teachers' fault, because all those teachers in all those other years can't be wrong—can they? Charlie doesn't know how to articulate his problem to his teachers, but he needs someone to mentor him as an intellectual risk-taker—as a creative thinker—or his narrow, pragmatic abilities will serve him less and less well as he moves further and further toward a time in his life when single right answers are of less and less value. He needs teachers who raise the bar for success and then help him learn how to succeed at those new and higher levels of intellect.

These nine profiles are of real middle school students—not made-up ones. Every one of them is either a high-performing or a high potential young adolescent, yet every one of them struggles in some way. Each of them needs teachers who understand both his or her potential and insecurities. Each of them needs middle school teachers who can help build bridges to becoming what he or she might be.

Principles Guiding Quality Classrooms

Our experiences as middle level educators and researchers suggest to us that teachers who are shepherds of possibility for these students will operate from several key principles that are important for all middle level students and then make modifications based on the particular needs of the diverse population of students who are academically advanced or have the potential to be. Such key principles include

- Early adolescence is a unique developmental stage and calls for teachers and classrooms that are responsive to the characteristics and needs of learners in that developmental stage.
- Young adolescents have many talents and abilities—both evident and dormant. The most effective middle grades teachers are continuously on the lookout for both kinds.
- Effective middle school teachers craft learning environments, curriculum, and instruction to help each learner develop self-esteem and move from a sense of self-worth to a sense of self-efficacy.
- High quality, challenging curriculum is important in helping students maximize their potential.
- Flexible and informed instruction is imperative in addressing the variety of learner needs that typify a middle level classroom.
- Every adolescent with talent, be it evident or dormant, will have areas of learning that require support and scaffolding, as well as areas that need to be stretched.
- Instructional approaches make a difference in addressing both the cognitive and affective needs of young adolescents.

Each of these principles is important for the success of virtually every young adolescent in our schools—including those with advanced ability or high potential. How teachers might apply the principles in general, and how teachers might apply the principles to address the needs of high-performing and high potential students is the focus of the next six chapters of this book. ❖

Learn More About Young Adolescent Development

Bowers, R. (2000). Young adolescent and emotional development: A constructivist perspective. In Wavering, M. (Ed.) *Educating young adolescents: Life in the middle*, 79–109. New York: Garland.

Csikzentmihalyi, M., Rathunde, K., & Whalen, W. (1993). *Talented teenagers: The roots of success and failure.* New York: Cambridge University Press.

Ford, D. (1996). *Reversing underachievement among gifted black students: Promising practices and programs.* New York: Teachers College Press.

Jensen, E. (2005). *Teaching with the brain in mind* (2nd Ed). Alexandria, VA: Association for Supervision and Curriculum Development.

Nelson, C. (2004). Brain development during puberty and adolescence: Comments on Part II. *Annals of the New York Academy of Sciences, 1021,* 105–109.

Rogers, K. (2002). *Reforming gifted education: How parents and teachers can match the program to the child.* Scottsdale, AZ: Great Potential Press.

Schave, D., & Schave, B. (1989). *Early adolescence and the search for self: A developmental perspective.* New York: Praeger.

2

The Role of Learning Environment in Developing and Extending Ability

The learning environment in a classroom is intangible, largely invisible, and easy for a teacher to relegate to the list of things to think about when there's time. Nonetheless, every classroom, for better or worse, has a learning environment—a tone—that signals students about "how it's going to be in here for me." The teacher is the architect of the learning environment, and it speaks unmistakably of the teacher's style of leadership, philosophy of teaching, and feelings about learners and learning.

To some degree, the learning environment directly mirrors the personality of the teacher. Is this going to be a lively place or a dour one? Will people act from a sense of obligation or opportunity? Is the classroom going to function like a monarchy or a democracy? Most teachers get better over time at understanding the classroom as a microcosm of a larger world and become more adept at creating, in that microcosm, the sorts of messages and experiences that help students learn about things like trust, respect, responsibility, and self-reflection.

The many elements of effective classroom environments are relatively universal in importance. That is, they matter when learners are in the primary grades, when they are young adolescents, and in higher education. They matter because they address human needs that may "change shape" over time, but do not go away. Positive learning environments are those that provide opportunities for students to experience

- Security
- Affirmation
- Affiliation
- Affinity
- High expectations
- Support
- Opportunity
- Power
- Purpose

We'll take a brief look at the meaning of each of these interrelated elements, then examine why each may be of particular importance in the middle grades. Finally, we'll look at ways in which each element might make a difference for students with high ability or high potential. The elements themselves don't change between grade levels, but ways teachers think about them, structure them, and apply them will be somewhat different in middle school than in kindergarten. Similarly, the elements don't change whether a student struggles in school, is a highly able learner, or both—but how the teacher thinks about the elements, structures them, and applies them may change in response to a student's particular experiences and needs.

Elements in Successful Classroom Environments

Security. The need for safety and security is one of the most fundamental human needs. By virtue of age, young people live in a world that is "too big" for their experiences. They don't have the capacity to control much that goes on around them; therefore, they need the places in which they spend the majority of their time to have a sense of safety and order. They need both physical and psychological safety. They need predictable routines and rules that help them function successfully and that protect them from the whims of others. Young learners need to know that classroom structures will protect and guide them. Without that assurance, students will avert much of the mental energy they should use for learning to self-protection.

Affirmation. As human beings, we also need to know we are acceptable to and accepted by those with whom we share significant time and space. This, too, is a kind of psychological safety. We want to know that important people in our lives find us worthy of their time, attention, and trust. Certainly, all human beings do things that should not be affirmed, but there's a difference in who we are and what we do. Each student needs to know that her teachers believe that she is one of the most important persons to enter the classroom each day. No student learns well who feels invisible, inconvenient, odd, or out of step. Not only must teachers signal that they value each student in the classroom, but they must also systematically signal the need for students to regard one another in that way as well.

> ## *No student learns well who feels invisible, inconvenient, odd, or out of step.*

Affiliation. Beyond feeling safe and valued in the classroom, students need to feel like they belong—like they are part of the group, part of the team. Each student comes to see his or her role in the class and to understand that the class would be diminished without the role that each student plays in shaping the group. At that point, the student starts to see himself or herself as part of something larger than self.

Affinity. Affiliation expands to affinity when students begin to see that other people in the group like or care about the same things they like and care about. In positive classroom environments, that plays out on two levels. First, there is opportunity for the student to connect with people who share common interests, concerns, experiences, and dreams. That not only affirms his or her ideas as valuable, but it provides a source for extending or amplifying those ideas as well. Second, the class as a whole—including the teacher—is enriched by learning from the perspectives of others. Through such perspective sharing, the members of the community not only expand their horizons, but also continue to develop respect for the unique worth of each community member.

High expectations. Affirmation and affinity build self-esteem, and without it, we are weakened as learners and people. However, to become what we might become, we have to move from self-esteem to self-efficacy. Self-esteem stems from the belief that we are worthwhile in the eyes of others. Self-efficacy means we know we can do important things. It begins when significant people in our lives set goals with and for us that we believe to be beyond our reach. The role of high expectations in classrooms cannot be overstated. High expectations are not glib rhetoric, but rather a teacher's highly personalized statement to a student that says, "This is something you've never accomplished. It's important, and you're going to accomplish it now, despite the fact that you think it's impossible for you." It's good to be valued as you are; it's even more significant to know important people believe you can become something better than you are. Self-efficacy is fostered by others who set high goals and expectations and supply the support necessary to reach these ideals.

> ## High expectations should always be presented in the context of high support.

Support. High expectations should always be presented in the context of high support. We learn that when we are presented with something to do that's a bit beyond our reach, others will help us extend our reach to accomplish it. In a positive learning environment, the teacher says to students individually and as a group, "Here's something huge and important for you to do. I know you can do it." The next part of the message is critical—"I know, because you're capable and because your classmates and I are going to be a part of your success." The implicit message is that people generally don't master really difficult things with ease; therefore, we have to persist—but in this classroom you won't be alone. You have a team of folks committed to your success and willing to be partners in your success. Support is non-negotiable in a high expectations classroom. Self-efficacy begins when someone helps us see beyond our visions for ourselves, but it actually occurs when we accomplish what we once believed was beyond our grasp. High expectations without high support have the opposite effect. In the absence of support, students fall short of the goal and learn that their doubts about their capacity were, in fact, correct.

Opportunity. For a young person to exceed his or her sense of possibility, an adult has to offer opportunities for that student to try out new roles. Of course, dynamic curriculum and instruction have much to do with opportunity making, but the classroom environment, too, should communicate that this is a place where students will see themselves in new roles. They will participate in making decisions, establishing rules, polishing routines, governing, being a colleague, decorating the classroom, and setting goals. The environment signals from the outset that this is the kind of place where students are consistently accorded responsibility that leads to opportunity.

Power. Outside of school, children learn eagerly, not because someone said they had to, but because it gives them increasing dominion or power in their world right away. In planning for school-based learning, we do well as teachers to ask ourselves, *Why should our students want to learn this? How will it empower them now as well in the future? How can I present these ideas and skills so that students readily see their utility in their lives?* Again, high quality curriculum and instruction play key roles in empowering students and thus tap their natural motivation to learn; the learning environment communicates messages to students about power they will derive from a classroom. Will they play key roles in operating the classroom? Will they be active decision makers and have choices about how to do what needs doing? Will others hear and listen to their voices? Does someone recognize in them something worth attending to? Is this classroom a place that expands their capacities? And don't forget to ask your students about those situations in which they feel powerful or powerless.

Purpose. Related to power is a sense of purpose in the classroom. Human beings, including young adolescents, are willing to invest in purposeful causes. For instance, in regard to curriculum, students tend to like subjects they believe can make a difference in people's lives. In regard to learning environment, wise teachers are purveyors of purpose as well. They help students understand that the classroom is a place where dreams are born and nurtured, or where every student is expected to grow to the max, or where taking risks is valued more than "playing it safe," or where we're all made richer by one another's insights, or where people ask and answer questions that matter to them, or where every student will be a thinker, or where student creativity is non-negotiable. There are many worthwhile purposes on which a teacher may elect to focus. They are likely to evolve as the teacher develops professionally and personally and in response to the corporate and individual needs of students. It is, however, the teacher's job to signal purpose to students, to involve them in discovering its value, to remind them of its impact on them as the year progresses. Purpose is a kind of glue that binds students together toward a common end. It makes a group of disparate individuals into an "us," and it helps students' willingness to invest in the hard work of learning and living together effectively.

> *Purpose is a kind of glue that binds students together toward a common end.*

These nine elements are important to most humans in most learning environments. Based on your perspectives and experiences, you may have others you want to add to the list. The list is not exclusive, but rather signals important precursors to the persistently risky but critical act of learning to build substantial lives.

Environmental Elements and Young Adolescents

Because young adolescents share basic needs with all other humans, they benefit from classroom environments that reflect security, affirmation, affiliation, affinity, high expectations, support, opportunity, power, and purpose. Because of their particular developmental stage, however, the elements take on added significance related to developmental tasks of early adolescence. Teachers who understand how the particular elements relate to issues, concerns, and needs of young adolescents have insights about how to present, craft, discuss, modify, and extend the elements in ways that benefit their learners.

Figure 1 capsules some ways in which the nine elements are salient to early adolescence and suggests some ways in which teachers might implement the elements in middle grades classrooms. The implementation suggestions include both general learning environment ideas as well as suggestions related to curriculum and instruction. The examples are also only a few of many possible ways to enact or implement each element.

Figure 1

Environmental Element	Significance in Young Adolescent Development	Suggestions for Implementation
1. Security	— Young adolescents often feel insecure about themselves because of rapid physical, emotional, and intellectual changes. Middle school is a step up from elementary school in terms of responsibility and autonomy; its structural and procedural changes can also provoke anxiety.	— Make sure the classroom looks "user friendly" to students. — Greet each student as he or she enters the classroom every day. — Establish and practice routines for starting class, stopping class, handing out materials, and moving among groups. — Use rubrics or checklists for success so that students have clear targets for their work.
2. Affirmation	— Young adolescents can feel awkward and vulnerable. They are a work in progress and need to know they are valuable, even if unfinished. — Young adolescents are in an important stage of identity formation and need to see learning as "belonging to" people of their gender, race, economic status, and culture.	— Make sure students continually see your respect for every student and see you insist on every student's respectful response to every other student. — Use materials that represent contributions of varied cultures, languages, races, genders to a subject. — Spotlight genuine accomplishments and significant growth of individuals and small groups. — Use dialogue journals so that students can communicate with the teacher. — Develop tasks that call on the strengths of individuals.
3. Affiliation	— Young adolescents have a strong need to affiliate with a peer group as they seek to define themselves somewhat separately from parents and other adults. — Young adolescents benefit from identification with a peer group that values individual strengths and achievement.	— Help classes develop a group identity, tasks, and projects that call for teamwork. — Use positive humor. — Create class stories and memories. — Help students work as a group to contribute as a group to the welfare of others.

continued

FIGURE 1

Environmental Element	Significance in Young Adolescent Development	Suggestions for Implementation
3. Affiliation (continued)		— Help students learn to identify their own strengths and those of peers. — Develop learning experiences that draw on multiple student strengths for successful completion. — Talk about individual and group successes and help the class celebrate them.
4. Affinity	— Young adolescents are in a time of exploration and development of interests and abilities. — Young adolescents need to develop positive peer networks.	— Use interest-based work groups as often as possible so that students can work with peers who have similar interests. — Introduce students to varied ways to express what they are learning and allow them choices for doing so. — Use analogies based on student interests to help explain and show real-world applications of what you are teaching.
5. High Expectations	— Young adolescents are dreamers, ready to conquer the world. — The young adolescent brain is at an important point of readiness to learn the skills of abstraction, critical thinking, and logical reasoning. — Young adolescents who tackle and succeed with high-level curriculum will be far more likely to continue on productive learning paths than those who work with low-level, "remedial," or rote learning.	— Teach all students the big ideas and skills of the disciplines so that they understand how the disciplines work and why. — Make sure all students consistently work at high levels of thought and reasoning, with consistent guidance in how to do so with increasing effectiveness. — Avoid "unacceptable" columns and descriptors on rubrics. Begin with what is acceptable and move up from there. — Have regular class discussions to evaluate how routines are working and to improve their effectiveness for everyone.

FIGURE 1

Environmental Element	Significance in Young Adolescent Development	Suggestions for Implementation
6. Support	— Young adolescents need adults to show them how to succeed at a new level and to provide emotional support for persisting when work is difficult. — Young adolescents benefit both academically and affectively from work with peers.	— Provide scaffolding (such as reading support, small-group instruction, teaching key academic vocabulary as a unit begins) to ensure that students for whom learning is more difficult have support for reaching important goals rather than allowing them to work for lesser goals. — Work with students in small groups to strengthen key areas of academic need rather than letting deficiencies slide. — Use a variety of student groupings for application of ideas and skills, peer review of important work, and studying.
7. Opportunity	— Young adolescents are eager to see themselves in new and positive ways. They need opportunities to "try on" varied possible roles. — Young adolescents typically know only a limited slice of what the world has to offer them. They are ready to explore a world much bigger than the one they have known.	— Assign students responsibility for all facets of classroom operation that they can manage. — Develop tasks and products that call on students to be involved with community members. — Develop products and tasks that address needs in the community and the world and draw on the widest possible range of talents and skills.
8. Power	— While young adolescents want to change the world, they are keenly aware that they are not yet ready to face the world. — Young adolescents need to separate themselves from the degree of adult "control" that characterizes the pre-teen years and need to develop the habits of mind that will allow them to do so safely and successfully.	— Develop curriculum that helps students relate to key themes in history, literature, art, music, and other subjects. — Ensure that students learn and use skills of critical thought, inquiry, and planning. — Develop tasks and products that enable students to teach younger students or help people beyond the classroom. — Help students learn to set, monitor, and assess goals important to them.

FIGURE 1 (con't.)

Environmental Element	Significance in Young Adolescent Development	Suggestions for Implementation
9. Purpose	— Young adolescents can be self-absorbed and benefit both from deepening insights about themselves and from reaching beyond themselves. — Young adolescents can be easily distracted and benefit from work that captures their interest.	— Develop curriculum that helps students make meaning of the disciplines rather than emphasizing rote learning. — Routinely share your thoughts about teaching with your students and engage them in discussions about teaching and learning. — Develop curriculum that encourages students to investigate real-world problems and issues and understand how adults use the knowledge, understanding, and skill they are learning.

Environmental Elements and Young Adolescents With High Performance or High Potential

Just as the fundamental elements of positive learning environments have the potential to address the particular needs of young adolescents, they also have the potential to address specific needs of students who are also "different" in their ability or potential. We often think of bright kids as "having it made" in school—after all, they get good grades. The truth is, however, that it's hard to grow up—no matter who you are. Being smart or having high potential does not exempt 10- to 15-year-olds from the difficulties inherent in the middle school years. In some ways, advanced ability or potential can actually contribute to the angst of being a young teen. Further, being smart or having high potential doesn't mean kids don't need teachers to play active roles in their learning and in their lives. They are *not* the kids "we don't need to worry about" because "they'll be fine on their own." In fact, if these students are to develop their capacities, they *absolutely* require teachers as partners—just as all other students do.

> *Being smart or having high potential does not exempt 10- to 15-year-olds from the difficulties inherent in the middle school years.*

So what are some of the ability-related issues high ability and high potential students may have in the years of early adolescence? There are many such issues. Some smart kids experience a number of them and some experience only a few. It's a rare student who escapes early adolescence without some bumps and bruises related to being highly able, a young adolescent, or both. Below are a few relatively common issues high-achieving young adolescents can encounter, followed by some issues common to that group. As the book continues, we'll examine additional ways in which middle school teachers can address these needs.

Some ability-related issues for high-achieving young adolescents

Needing both to achieve and to belong. For many young adolescents, it becomes fashionable, for a time, to thumb one's nose at school as something only adults value. For these students, it's more interesting to invest in friends, e-mail, and text-messaging. It's almost fashionable to devalue school—at least on the surface. It's a part of bonding with peers in the same way that kids bond by disparaging school cafeteria food or curfew rules. For students whose identity is closely bound to academic achievement, however, to reject school is to reject what the student has represented and embraced for years; this further compounds the identity issues inherent in early adolescence. On the other hand, these students, too, long to have friends and to be part of a peer group. Some bright young adolescents feel like they have to reject achievement to have friends or give up friends to continue achieving. Either decision is very costly. Very bright students need teachers who understand the importance of both achieving *and* belonging and who help develop classroom environments in which the two needs are highly compatible.

Coping with "uneven" development. It is often the case that a very bright middle school student thinks much more like an adult than a 12-year-old. At the same time, the student may be very small physically and thus be treated like a child. Other bright middle schoolers may get every math problem right but have no idea how to make friends; their intellect is advanced but their social skills are not. In early adolescence, it is important to nearly all students—including very bright ones—to have friends. Highly able learners may also suffer with "uneven development" when their teachers (generally unconsciously) conclude that because they are bright, they should act like they are much older all the time and are harsh when they sometimes become the young adolescents they are emotionally, socially, or behaviorally. These students need adults in their lives who understand that it is possible to be very advanced in some areas, "on target" in others, and behind the curve in others and who accept students with those uneven developmental patterns and help them understand themselves.

Living with heightened sensitivity. Some (not all) bright middle schoolers are highly sensitive to events in the world or in their school. They suffer when they see injustice around them. They worry about children who go to bed hungry at night. They feel as though they are responsible for "fixing" the world's inequities. At the same time, they are frustrated because they feel incapable of making a difference. They lack the means and the skills to solve the problems that occupy their thinking. It is as though they have the sensitivities of a wise adult and the capacities of a child—a very uncomfortable position. Very bright and highly sensitive young adolescents need teachers who are aware and respectful of their sensitivities, who give them opportunities to explore their concerns, and who help them find appropriate ways to take action related to those concerns, when feasible. In these ways, they develop a sense that they can help solve the problems that trouble them.

Pursuing perfection. A good number of very able students ride the crest of perfect grades throughout elementary school. They (and their parents) enter middle school with the mindset that to make less than straight As is to fail. In truth, perfection is both an unattainable and an unhealthy goal; but typically these students have never had to struggle with schoolwork. If middle school is appropriately challenging for them, there will be times when they cannot guarantee an "A" performance. Again, the student's self-concept is threatened, and different students respond to this in different ways. Some students give up on themselves. Some get angry at teachers. Some continue a relentless pursuit of grades and beat themselves up emotionally when they cannot live up to the standards they have set for themselves. Perfectionism can also lead to habitual procrastination, eating disorders, and sometimes even suicide. Bright young adoelscents need adults who can help them learn to pursue *excellence* rather than *perfection* in their lives—and that begins by understanding the difference between the two.

Lacking effective study skills. It seems odd that kids who have been very successful academically would lack study skills, but it's a relatively common problem in the adolescent years. Because many very bright kids consistently do schoolwork that is designed for students with less advanced understanding and skill, they can often make good grades by simply listening in class, completing homework they already know how to do, and turning in projects they created on "automatic pilot," but that nonetheless look better than those of other students. At whatever point in their school experience work becomes challenging, bright students can find themselves largely unprepared to cope with the challenge. Dissecting text may be necessary for the first time. Both the volume and complexity of work may seem overwhelming. Persisting in the face of continuing uncertainty about solutions to problems is not only unfamiliar, but very uncomfortable. While highly able students can certainly learn to study effectively, the point is that they have to learn. They'll benefit from teachers who understand both the practical and emotional challenges of "learning to climb a higher mountain" and who help them develop the skills and attitudes necessary to succeed at a level of challenge that's more appropriate for their advanced ability.

Hungering to learn more. Very bright middle schoolers often have minds that hunger to learn in the same way that a talented athlete hungers to spend time on the athletic field or in the gym. It is often the case that these students read and think about very adult issues and problems in world events, math, science, anthropology, astronomy, and so on. Because their minds are more adult-like than childlike, they may find grade level work stultifying. At a time when it is very important for young people to find learning energizing, a consistent menu of under-nourishing academic fare leaves them disenchanted, frustrated, or angry. The place that *should* represent learning, ironically, seems like a fraud to them. They literally feel like they are starving to death intellectually. Very bright young adolescents need adults who help them feed their minds.

> *Very bright middle schoolers often have minds that hunger to learn in the same way that a talented athlete hungers to spend time on the athletic field or in the gym.*

Feeling different. Early adolescence is a time when fitting in matters greatly. Students at this age may struggle if they feel different because they don't have the right clothes, or the standard haircut, or get braces before peers, or wear glasses, or are too big or too little. It just doesn't sell well to stick out during the early teen years. Being too smart can also feel alienating for very bright kids if they feel alone in their ability. Kids may roll their eyes when a very bright learner asks a question. The highly able student gets teased for making good grades or for not making good grades. To be smart is to be a geek, and who wants *that* label? Very bright young adolescents need teachers who doggedly cultivate environments in which all students learn to respect others' unique contributions—including high academic ability.

Being good in too many areas. While excelling in many areas might seem like anything but a problem, it can, in fact, present real conflicts for very bright young adolescents. At a time when middle schoolers are beginning to envision themselves in the future, these students can find themselves pulled in many directions. For example, the science teacher says Josh should definitely prepare himself for a career in medicine, physics, or a related field. His grandfather says he has the mind of a lawyer and not-so-secretly hopes he'll join the family law practice. Josh's music teacher says he's seldom seen a student who has such an ear for musical composition at such a young age and has featured two of his compositions at the spring concert. Josh's math teacher has recommended him for a scholarship for a summer math program at a university in a neighboring state. Josh loves writing and keeps a very active blog of his poetry and essays. No matter where he turns, someone seems to see him in a role that is not at all clear to him. He's afraid he'll let someone down no matter what choices he makes. The pressure seems heavy, and he has no idea how to make the right decisions about his future. Very bright students need teachers who help them explore possibilities while providing assurance that it's okay not to be sure exactly what you want to do with your life when you're 12. They need teachers who help them "window-shop" for possibilities without pressure to "buy."

Some ability-related issues for high potential young adolescents

Being unaware of their own possibilities. Many students who have great, untapped potential are not fully aware of that fact themselves. Some will say they knew they were smart but didn't know what to do about it. Some see themselves as leaders of peers, exerting either positive or negative leadership, but don't connect that with "school smarts." Typically, however, these students have not received excellent grades, the highest test scores, or awards for achievement. Educators have not sent the signals that typically go to very able learners. Parents may not have been fully involved in school. It's likely that their closest friends are not very high achievers. Thus, it's not surprising that these young people do not readily see themselves as smart kids or at least not as kids with school smarts. It is critically important that teachers of these middle schoolers recognize their abilities, share that recognition with them, and actively support the recognition and affirmation of their potential.

Feeling alienated from school and academics. Often high potential students feel at odds with school. They may come from low-income backgrounds and may not have access to the tools that school may take for granted—for example, computers, reference books, supplies, and readily available transportation. They may come from cultural groups other than Caucasian and may see that their school does not mirror their heritage in the holidays and heroes it celebrates, the history it teaches, the classroom examples it offers, the ethnicity of its teachers or in its high status student organizations, high-end classes, and student body leaders. Further, for many such students, peers can exert considerable pressure to opt out of meaningful participation in the institution of school and what it represents. At the same time, the content of school in the middle grades may seem very detached from the world to which many high potential, underperforming students return at night. For many reasons, school just doesn't score. For these students, it makes a great difference to have middle school teachers who work tenaciously to make the classroom alive, dynamic, and connected to their students' lives.

Lacking gatekeeper knowledge, experiences, and skills. Because the high potential of some students often goes unrecognized, many of these students enter middle school already at a disadvantage. They have not seen themselves as serious students and have not learned to study effectively and systematically. Many come to middle school lacking key academic vocabulary. They have typically not been in advanced classes or "high" groups; and for that reason, they have not been "groomed" for advanced math, foreign language, and critical thinking in the middle grades. They may not have school-savvy parents who have made sure they participate in school or extracurricular experiences that pave the way for high achievement. By the middle grades, these students are not only likely to feel they don't "belong" among high achievers, in fact, they are already at a clear deficit for academic success without serious adult intervention and support. They have a critical need for teachers who actively teach them how to succeed and how to develop the mindset, attitudes, and skills necessary for high achievement.

Feeling pulled in conflicting directions. In addition to the pull of peers, which may run counter to the pull of academics, high potential, underperforming young adolescents may feel pulled in conflicting directions for other reasons as well. In some instances, parents "push" them to do well academically, while peers send the opposite message. In other cases, the students themselves want to be successful in school, and their teachers encourage that success; but heavy home responsibilities or parent messages to the contrary make that goal a steep climb. Unfortunately, it is still the case that girls, in particular, may be discouraged in their homes or neighborhoods from aspiring to high academic achievement. Some students struggle with knowing more English than their parents and the power imbalance that can follow. They may already understand that achieving at high academic levels can separate a young person from family in significant ways. At a time in life when it seems that even one's own body sends mixed signals, it is very difficult for students who also receive conflicting messages from many other corners of their lives about navigating academic success. They need middle school teachers to help them learn to live in two worlds—to respect family, peers, and cultures that are central to their lives and also to respect and comfortably navigate a world of expanding possibilities.

Lacking a road map to the future. High potential, underperforming young adolescents are certainly old enough to begin to connect important dots about the future: *People who do well in school go on to college. College costs a lot of money and my family has no money. Nobody in my family has ever been to college before. I can't leave home. I need to get a job to help out at home. Besides, nobody I know even knows how to go about getting into college. This high achievement stuff is not for me. It's a dead-end street.* Sadly, there are many high potential young adolescents who believe that a high quality education makes a difference in one's future but that it is not a viable option for them. These students need adults who help them see academics as part of their future, who help them understand the means of accessing academic opportunities, and who will be their partners in gaining that access in the short-term and the long-term.

Lacking a support system. It is likely that many high potential, underperforming middle schoolers will fail to reach their potential without a consistent, persistent, insistent support system to help them do so. The challenges they would have to surmount to grow into their potential are many. They need peers who also have aspirations to do great things, who understand the cost, and who will hang in with them for the duration of the journey. They need adults who believe in them and regularly articulate that belief over an extended period. They need adults who will help them study "backwards and forwards" at the same time—in other words, adults who help them work at high levels of challenge while helping them "fill in the gaps" to overcome deficits in their knowledge, understanding, and skill. They need adults who oversee homework regularly and help them find and take advantage of out-of-school opportunities that broaden their aspirations and abilities. They need opportunities to understand the options that exist for them as adults in the world, and they need a tenacious support network to guide them to possible futures.

Fearing stereotype threat. For some young adolescents with high potential and less impressive achievement, academic success is further hampered by the sense that many people in their world don't believe that "people like them" are smart. Stemming from a long history of both overt and covert messages from institutions, media, and individuals, such students may conclude that teachers, more privileged peers, principals, and counselors believe students who are poor, Black, Hispanic, Native American, and so on aren't capable of high academic performance. Thus, in addition to the other significant barriers to achievement these students face, they have a clear sense that their economic status, ethnicity, or race triggers negative assumptions in significant adults about their ability to succeed. Research suggests their conclusions regarding these assumptions are often well-founded. Further, it suggests that even when influential adults do not view them in stereotypically negative ways, they may under-perform, nonetheless, because of their fear that they are seen as academically less capable than other students. These young adolescents don't need "color blind" teachers but rather teachers who examine their own experiences and biases, who respect and feel enriched by students' varied backgrounds, and who insist upon and support each student's continued growth toward the highest possible academic performance.

> *Our "sense of students" develops as we grow professionally; and teachers who invest in understanding their students will have an increasingly richer sense of what it means to be a young adolescent.*

What's a Middle School Teacher To Do?

To say that teaching middle schoolers is a complex task defines the concept of understatement. Every middle school student has a complicated and multifaceted life that evolves daily. In addition, middle school teachers typically teach too many students to know each of them broadly and deeply. While we cannot know and understand all of our students as fully as we might like, we can know and understand each student better when we set out to do so than when we give up because of the immensity of the task. Further, our "sense of students" develops as we grow professionally; and teachers who invest in understanding their students will have an increasingly richer sense of what it means to be a young adolescent—one with a learning disability, one who is very tall, one who is learning to speak Spanish, or one who is a high achiever. This insight deepens with every meaningful moment we spend with students; hence, our sense of students is infinitely richer over time. We can study and "learn" our students in the same ways we study and learn the content we teach.

Essential Considerations

The remainder of the book will provide suggestions for understanding high ability and high potential young adolescents more fully and for teaching them more successfully. For now, consider the following assertions to see if they align with your beliefs:

1. **Every middle school student brings to school a unique and valuable life.**
2. **Every one of those lives is complicated because human beings are complicated, more so because early adolescence is a very complicated time of life.**
3. **Every young adolescent life is also complicated by individual factors—being too tall or too short, too thin or too heavy, having too many friends or not enough, being too timid or too bold, having parents who don't pay enough attention or who pay too much attention, struggling in school or being very smart, being too aware of one's abilities or being unaware of them, and on and on. The list is long and indicative of the immense value of adults who can help young people find balance.**
4. **Every young adolescent needs teachers who believe in him or her and who live out that belief daily—even when the student stops believing.**
5. **High ability students are not exempt from being human, being early adolescents, being in search of a sound life. They also are not exempt from needing teachers to help them build such a life. Middle school is a pivotal time to help such students solidify their passions for learning and the attitudes that can make those passions worthy of a lifetime pursuit.**
6. **High potential, underperforming students are not exempt from any of those things, either. They are, however, at considerable risk of not building the lives that would most fulfill them and most benefit society. They have a special need for teachers who look beyond the surface and help students give birth to dreams and build ladders to reach those dreams. Middle school is the last best hope for many of these students as they begin to crystallize who they will be as adults.**

In the end, we believe that great middle school teachers are searchers for talent, developers of talent, and advocates for talent. We believe all that begins with a commitment to "tuning in" to each student who comes our way, continues with a commitment to building a learning environment that daily welcomes each student into a learning community, and proceeds with a commitment to use what we teach and how we teach to dignify and extend the possibilities in each young person we teach. ❖

Learn More About the Importance of Learning Environment and Affect in Teaching High Ability and High Potential Learners

Beane, J. A. & Lipka, R. P. (1986). *Self-concept, self-esteem, and the curriculum.* New York: Teachers College Press.

Boykin, A. (2000). The talent development model of schooling: Placing students at promise for academic success. *Journal of Education for Students Placed at Risk, 5*(1&2), 3–25.

Ginsberg, M., & Wlodkowski, R. (2000). *Creating highly motivating classrooms for all students: A schoolwide approach to powerful teaching with diverse learners.* San Francisco: Jossey-Bass.

Perry, T., Steele, C., & Hilliard, A. (2003). *Young, gifted, and black: Promoting high achievement among African-American students.* Boston: Beacon.

Tatum, B. (1997). *Why are all the Black kids sitting together in the cafeteria? And other conversations about race.* New York: Basic Books.

Tomlinson, C. (2004). *Fulfilling the promise of the differentiated classroom: Strategies and tools for responsive teaching.* Alexandria, VA: Association for Supervision and Curriculum Development.

Tomlinson, C., Ford, D., Reis, S., Briggs, C., & Strickland, C. (2004). *In search of the dream: Designing schools and classrooms that work for high potential students from diverse cultural backgrounds.* Washington, DC: National Association for Gifted Children.

Walters, L. (2002). Latino achievement reexamined. *Harvard Education Letter, 7,* 9-11.

3

The Role of Curriculum in Developing and Extending Ability

Who am I?
I am a powder keg—
Anger building until someone
Makes it explode. ...
I am an eraser—
Eliminating all the bad thoughts from my head
I am an ant—
Everyone looks down on me
I am nothing—
No one can see me
But I am something—
Brilliant and intelligent
Who am I?
Powder keg...eraser, ant, nothing, and something—
These are the things I think about
In my everyday life.
I am me.

—April, 7th Grade

arly adolescence is a time of intensive self-examination and self-discovery as well as a critical period of socialization. These developmental truths hold enormous possibility and promise for educators who seek to help young adolescents discover and extend their abilities—but they can throw up barriers as well. High ability and high potential middle grades students must decide whether they are going to commit to developing their potential or disengage from its cultivation in favor of more appealing options. The nature of the curriculum with which these students work daily may well be a "swing vote" in this pivotal decision. Teachers who develop curriculum that helps young adolescents understand themselves and the world around them in ways that are mentally energizing do more than "teach well"; they are catalysts for student investment in a fulfilling future.

We believe strongly that the foundation of effective curriculum for high-performing and high potential adolescents is also the foundation of effective curriculum for virtually all young adolescents. Very able learners are unlikely to be captivated by or to invest deeply in a curriculum of drill and practice—but neither are most other young adolescents. Very able learners are not drawn to curriculum that demands memorization of information that makes little sense to them and appears to have little purpose—but neither are most other young adolescents. Very able learners don't benefit a great deal from curriculum that seems detached from their world and from their interests—but neither do most other young adolescents.

> *The foundation of effective curriculum for high-performing and high potential adolescents is also the foundation of effective curriculum for virtually all young adolescents.*

Highly able middle schoolers may have less tolerance than some other peers for classrooms with these characteristics because, in some ways, they are "connoisseurs" of quality curriculum; tolerant or not, however, middle school students in general don't derive much benefit from such curriculum. Highly able middle schoolers may suffer more in the short term than some other peers from such classrooms because high ability students in these classrooms are not only asked to learn things that lack meaning for them but are also asked to spend time "learning" what they already know (or could learn rapidly). Nonetheless, few middle schoolers are likely to reap long-term benefits from such curriculum.

Key Characteristics of Quality Curriculum in the Middle Grades

Decades of studying how students learn and the characteristics of curriculum that maximizes learning suggests that there are at least seven non-negotiable and interrelated characteristics of quality curriculum for high-performing and high potential middle level learners. It is really only the seventh characteristic that speaks directly to the special needs of high-performing and high potential middle schoolers, however. The other characteristics may be particularly important for students with advanced ability, but they are also very important to the development of all middle schoolers and reflect research and practice related to quality middle level curriculum in general.

1. High quality middle level curriculum is developmentally appropriate. Effective middle grades curriculum helps students make sense of themselves and the world around them. At this developmental stage, students struggle to understand themselves, their relationships, and their world. Good curriculum helps them delve deeply into these areas of concern. The early adolescent brain seeks pleasure more than pain. Classrooms that emphasize rote learning inevitably evoke the battle cry, "How come we gotta learn this stuff?!"

Curriculum that attends to the very real-life concerns of the students who use it is more pleasurable and, thus, more likely to succeed in helping students learn what they need to learn. Such curriculum helps students make connections between essential content and those early adolescent questions: *Who am I? Why do I matter? How does the world make sense? How do we create a better environment? What can people do to make the world a more peaceful place? How can I play a role in making this a just and fair world? Are the lives of famous people at all like my life? How do other people solve conflicts? How do I find a voice?* Teachers who develop quality curriculum for young adolescents ensure that what they teach is meaningful and relevant to the adolescent brain, that it helps students discover and develop their own strengths and passions, that it establishes points of personal connection with students, and that it helps students see what they understand, care about, and can use in their world.

2. High quality middle level curriculum is organized around key concepts and essential understandings. Curriculum that is organized around key concepts and essential understandings is ideally positioned to help students grapple successfully with important developmental questions. Such curriculum is also essential in helping young adolescents set the stage for authentic, enduring understanding of the various academic disciplines. Much of what students memorize is ephemeral. The human brain (and particularly the young adolescent brain) is not a very effective or efficient memorizing machine. What students genuinely understand, by contrast, is long-lasting, transferable, and more easily applied. A student who truly understands math can think mathematically. A student who really understands how science functions can reason like a scientist. A student who genuinely "gets" the big ideas of history can think analytically about events beyond the pages of the social studies textbook. Concept-based curriculum creates a landscape in which young adolescents can exercise their growing capacity to think and reason with increasing degrees of abstraction.

> *Concept-based curriculum creates a landscape in which young adolescents can exercise their growing capacity to think and reason with increasing degrees of abstraction.*

Concepts are broad ideas (generally reflected in a single word) that reflect essential meaning of a topic or discipline as an expert in the discipline would see it. Concepts frame, organize, and unite the parts of information presented in curriculum that can otherwise seem disjointed to students. Concepts provide openings through which students can tunnel their way into the core of a discipline to discover its deep understandings, issues, and controversies. For example, a life science teacher could organize a unit or a course around the concept of "interdependence," asking students to explore ways in which changes in one part of a system (cell, ecosystem, food chain, human body, other) affect other parts of that system. Figure 2 shows other examples of important concepts in the disciplines.

FIGURE 2

Some Sample Concepts From Key Disciplines	
History:	*conflict,* scarcity, culture, system, region, rights and responsibilities
Literature:	voice, irony, theme, wisdom, figure of speech, *conflict,* perceptions
Science:	force, properties of matter, interaction, conflict, energy, adaptation, *system*
Music:	rhythm, tone, tempo, harmony, melody, *conflict,* dissonance, *pattern*
Mathematics:	balance, symmetry, probability, *pattern,* ratio, congruence
Art:	perspective, line, texture, space, color, *pattern,* expression, impressionism

Some concepts are central to several disciplines—note the italicized, recurring themes of conflict, system, and pattern in Figure 2. This overlap presents powerful opportunities to connect learning across subject areas, lending depth and meaning to multidisciplinary studies. In a concept-based interdisciplinary unit, the concept of study would remain constant across subjects, but the manner in which each discipline "unpacks" or investigates the concept would change according to the *essential understandings* of the different fields of study.

Essential understandings, also sometimes called big ideas, principles, or generalizations, are the "rules" or "truths" that govern the concepts or make them work like they do. For example, an essential understanding about the concept of interdependence is, "When one part of an interdependent *system* is strengthened, the whole *system* is likely to benefit." This particular essential understanding carries weight in several disciplines (e.g., governmental systems, ecosystems, essay composition, other). Other essential understandings may be more subject-specific. Figure 3 shows additional examples of essential understandings related to key concepts in the disciplines. The concept which each essential understanding helps to explain is in *boldface type.*

Figure 3

Some Sample Essential Understandings From Key Disciplines	
Social Studies:	*Change* can be both evolutionary and revolutionary.
Math:	*Measurement* expresses properties on a defined numerical scale.
Music:	Music communicates through the *conflict* and resolution of tonal patterns.
Science:	*Adaptation* allows animals to change themselves to meet their basic needs in a particular environment.
Literature:	Different *perspectives* of characters in a story generate conflict.
Art:	An artist interprets an event, belief, emotion, object, or idea through *expressive color.*

Curriculum that is organized around key concepts and essential understandings or principles helps all middle school students construct meaning from a deluge of facts and invites meaningful interdisciplinary teaching and learning. It is actually shared *concepts*—rather than *topics* —that unite disciplines in meaningful ways. Consider two examples of interdisciplinary middle school curricula. In one, students are studying the American Revolution in social studies. To create an interdisciplinary unit, teachers decided that students would paint murals of the American Revolution in art, sing songs from the time period in music, compare populations then and now using graphs in math, study common diseases of the time period in science, and read novels about the American Revolution in literature. Students may get a hefty dose and perhaps even a richer understanding of the American Revolution through that curriculum.

However, it is doubtful that they will develop more coherent or authentic views of the other disciplines through such a study. Everything in the unit is essentially *in service* of the social studies curriculum.

In a second middle school, teachers determined that the concepts of *patterns, conflict, interdependence, change, systems,* and *order* are authentic to all of their disciplines and the topics they plan to explore during the year. In each of their classes, they will guide students in examining how the five concepts work to help them understand and apply the content. At various times, they will also guide students in comparing and contrasting the principles or essential understandings they are developing about the concepts across subjects. Concept-based instruction not only provides teachers and students an opportunity to learn each discipline authentically but also to make comparisons across disciplines, to explore how understanding one discipline can help us understand others and, perhaps most importantly, to see how the disciplines connect to students' lives. After all, their lives provide prime examples of patterns, conflict, interdependence, change, systems, and order. In this way, concepts encourage natural connections within and across subjects and between content and student experiences. It is not difficult to see how those connections would readily occur in the example of the "interdisciplinary unit" based on the topic of the American Revolution in Figure 4.

FIGURE 4

Sample Interdisciplinary Connections Around the Concept of "Conflict"		
Subject	**Essential Understanding/Principle**	**Topics of Study**
Social Studies	Conflict in society produces both destruction and advancement.	Roman invasion, Civil War, civil rights, immigration
Language Arts	Characters grow and change as a result of conflict.	literature and composition
Science	Conflict in nature results in changes to both landscapes and inhabitants.	geology, adaptation, Ice Age, evolution
Math	The conflict of the "unknown" drives mathematicians to develop formulas in order to decode our world.	Pythagorean Theorem, geometry

For advanced students, concepts and essential understandings or principles provide a natural springboard for deeper or more expert-like exploration of content and help teachers avoid the inclination to "challenge" advanced students by giving them *more* work to do (rather than deeper or more complex work) or by assigning tangential tasks such as working on puzzles or creating games. We'll explore how this might work in Chapter 4.

3. High quality middle level curriculum is interwoven with the skills of student empowerment. Adolescents are growing in their ability to move beyond direct experience and into the realm of abstract reasoning. At the same time, they are ready for increasing independence and academic rigor. The middle school years, therefore, are a pivotal time for students to consistently use problem-solving skills, skills of independence, and other higher order thinking operations to understand content, make meaningful connections, and develop awareness of the power of their minds. Concept-based curriculum provides a natural setting for students to discover, explore, investigate, and construct knowledge, much as practitioners in a discipline would.

> *Concept-based curriculum provides a natural setting for students to discover, explore, investigate, and construct knowledge, much as practitioners in a discipline would.*

While most teachers want our students to be independent thinkers and problem solvers, we may not plan for students to develop these skills in the systematic ways necessary for students to develop competence and confidence with them. A full discussion on the kinds of skills that would empower young adolescents is beyond the scope of this book. Nonetheless, it is helpful to consider a sample of the categories and kinds of skills teachers should consider learning about and purposefully incorporating into curriculum. Figure 5 provides an extensive sampler.

FIGURE 5

Category of Skill	Examples of Skills in the Category	Ways Teachers Might Encourage Students to Develop the Skills
Skills of the Discipline	— **Math:** finding patterns, predicting, problem solving — **Science:** hypothesizing, observing, classifying, data analysis — **Literature:** analysis, interpretation — **History:** weighing evidence, detecting bias, determining reliable resources	— Determine the skills experts in the discipline use. — Design tasks and products that call on students to use those skills. — Teach students the names of the skills and descriptions of them. — Ensure that students have opportunities to watch and learn from experts at work. — Include criteria related to skills of the discipline in rubrics and checklists for success.
Skills of Independence	— Metacognition — Posing questions — Finding answers — Finding worthy resources — Prioritizing — Goal setting — Evaluating progress — Revising goals — Establishing criteria for success — Determining quality	— Assign students tasks that call for increasing skills of independence. — Discuss the skills with students. — Have students assess their current and growing competencies in the skills. — Monitor student readiness in the skills and ensure support necessary for students to grow from their current points of development. — Model the skills for students and talk about them in your life and work.
Critical Thinking Skills	— Comparing and contrasting — Detecting cause and effect — Seeing relationships — Analyzing — Synthesizing — Evaluating — Categorizing — Classifying — Sequencing — Distinguishing fact and opinion — Drawing conclusions — Generalizing — Recognizing bias	— Design tasks that require critical thinking. — Concentrate on a relatively small number of critical thinking skills key to your discipline. — Encourage students to talk aloud about how they are thinking when they use a particular skill. — Have students develop descriptions of steps in the various thinking processes. — Teach students key vocabulary of critical thinking. — Make sure students can name the kind of thinking called for by a task or problem and can understand why it is a productive kind of thinking for that problem.

continued

FIGURE 5

Category of Skill	Examples of Skills in the Category	Ways Teachers Might Encourage Students to Develop the Skills
Creative Thinking Skills	— Elaboration — Flexible thinking — Fluency — Brainstorming — Seeing and modifying attributes — Creative problem solving — Metaphorical thinking — Imagining — Innovating — Appreciating and creating humor	— Design open-ended tasks that incorporate important goals. — Teach the skills of creative thinking. — Help students see the various kinds of jobs, hobbies, and life situations that call for creative thinking. — Model creative thinking. — Draw student attention to the power of creative thinking in the world. — Introduce and study the work of famous creative thinkers. — Help students determine when to use creative vs. critical thinking and how to balance the two.
Productive Habits of Mind	— Persistence — Patience — Open-mindedness — Self-reflection — Working hard — Accepting and seeking positive critique — Seeking multiple viewpoints on a topic or issue — Striving for accuracy — Striving for quality	— Talk about habits of mind. — Model them. — Have students analyze how their habits of mind are contributing to their success. — Use rubric and checklist criteria related to habits of mind. — Guide students in studying, through biography, the habits of mind of eminent people in varied fields and from varied cultures.
Social-Affective Skills	— Listening — Empathizing — Accepting and valuing alternative points of view — Seeking consensus — Collaborating successfully — Being a good leader — Being a good group member	— Talk about these skills in regard to small-group work, individually, and for the class as a whole. — Make sure group tasks are appealing to students and draw on strengths of each student. — Model the traits yourself. — Help students look for positive and negative examples of the traits of people in the news.

FIGURE 5

Category of Skill	Examples of Skills in the Category	Ways Teachers Might Encourage Students to Develop the Skills
Basic Skills	— Analyzing text — Attending to directions — Setting up equations — Map reading — Mathematical writing — Reading charts and tables — Writing a well-developed essay — Communicating clearly	— Recognize that these are the fundamental skills in every subject. — Encourage students by showing them how these skills are best learned in contexts to do work they find interesting and important.

One way that Mrs. Abrams helps her English students develop skills of empowerment is to have them work with authentic writing tasks throughout the year. Students select topics or issues of interest to them and then pursue them in various genres. They meet in writing discussion groups to share both their writing and their writing processes, much as authors do. Mrs. Abrams guides them in developing language to talk about how they write and the quality of their content. As they read selections by various authors, she always has them explore authors as writers, comparing the professionals' writing experiences with their own. She helps the class understand the range of successful approaches used by real writers and by their peers. She also ensures that they develop expert level language for reflecting on their work and discussing it with others. She finds that this approach helps her students develop self-awareness as writers and a sense of control over the processes of writing. She easily embeds the requirements of state writing standards in the approach.

High quality middle level curriculum fosters connection and relevance.
Because young adolescents are eager to make sense of the world that surrounds them and the broader world they will eventually inherit, they are no longer satisfied with hand-me-down meaning, rules, and logic. Rather, they seek to find their own sense of things. At the same time, they are exploring relationships to figure out how to "fit" into a social scheme that extends beyond family. For those reasons, effective middle level teachers build into their curriculum "points of connection" that help

students see the utility of what they are learning in their everyday lives as well as in the world around them and that help them engage with peers in work that honors their growing potential as thinkers and problem solvers. There are many ways middle grades curriculum can be connective and relevant for students.

- When they discover how something they learned in one subject sheds important light on another, and when they see their skills as immediately useful and transferable, students are more likely to invest in the subject because it helps them make meaning and increase their sense of power as learners.
- When their work serves as a catalyst for positive group interaction and success, they are more likely to invest because that meets both an academic and social need.
- When curriculum calls on students to connect with adults beyond the classroom, investment increases because it helps the students explore the wider world in which they have increasing interest and envision possibilities for themselves in that world. Further, it helps them see how knowledge and skill contribute to something "real," and how knowledge and skill make sense in practical application.
- When curriculum calls on middle grades students to connect with younger students to enhance the learning and success of younger students, young adolescents learn more readily. Not only do they assume the role of teacher (which inevitably clarifies learning), but they also assume roles as leaders and people who can positively impact others.
- When curriculum connects with their individual interests, investment increases because the work is personally motivating.
- When curriculum connects with a student's cultural experiences, that student's investment is magnified because the work not only seems to "belong" to that individual but helps him or her understand learning in the context of his or her heritage.
- When curriculum connects with ways in which a student learns best, investment increases because the learning process is both more natural and more effective for the learner.

Early adolescence is prime time for making connections and finding relevance—with peers, with a broader slice of the world, with meaning, with self, and with the future. So powerful are these needs for connection in students of this age, that they dominate student energy and attention. High quality middle grades curriculum neither ignores nor fights against this inclination but rather seizes the opportunity it presents to help young learners see learning as a powerful means to the powerful ends they seek for continued development.

> *Early adolescence is prime time for making connections and finding relevance—with peers, with a broader slice of the world, with meaning, with self, and with the future.*

Mr. Lincoln consistently brings in articles and video clips that show students how science "makes the news" in a variety of ways. He also has three ongoing work groups in the class that students join to produce scientific products. One group is working on a book of biographies for upper elementary students on scientists of both genders that represent a wide range of cultural groups. Its goal is to help younger learners realize that people from around the world contribute to science and use it to benefit others. A second group is developing a series of computer animations that demonstrate key scientific processes. The goal is to provide students in future years clear ways of "seeing" what the processes really look like in action rather than only explained in the pages of the book. The third group is working on projects of the members' own choosing (with teacher approval) that relate to key content in the course about which they'd like to learn more. Students in that group may work alone or with a small group as they write their study proposal and carry it out. Students in all groups work on their investigations at teacher-designated times, when they finish assigned tasks, and often before and after school because they enjoy the work and the time with one another and with Mr. Lincoln. He finds that his students are much more invested in science now and that they make many more connections between course content and their interests than was the case in the past.

High quality middle level curriculum uses choice to help students discover the joy of learning. Choice is especially important to middle schoolers because of their changing roles in life. Sometimes for the first time, these students are making independent decisions and selecting courses of action available to them. Because students of this age are relatively new in handling significant choices at a more independent level, they are also vulnerable because of their lack of experience in this area.

When curriculum offers students choices about how to learn important goals, how to express their learning, and venues for applying what they learn, at least three positive outcomes are likely. First, providing students with meaningful choices dignifies their status as decision makers. Second, it enables teachers to work directly with students on what it means to make wise choices. Third, the choices enable students to focus their work on areas of budding interest or existing passion, which increases student interest and investment in the work.

Such choices should never enable students to circumvent essential knowledge, understanding, and skill; rather, they provide students alternative routes to learning what is essential and, thereby, increase the likelihood that a student will find satisfaction in the process, sustain motivation to learn, and realize academic success.

Ms. Bonetta tries to give her students choices as often as possible. She even lets them decide on the best day (within a range she provides) to turn in projects and take tests. She often allows them to decide whether to work on math tasks with a partner or alone. She holds optional mini-classes on topics that can be stumbling blocks for students or on math-related topics of interest to them. Students decide which of the mini-classes would be of value to them, individually, and attend those. Ms. Bonetta also sometimes has them recall aloud the key understandings and skills for a chapter and then says to them, "Based on your most recent work, if you feel you need most practice with the first skill, do homework assignment A. If you feel you need most practice with the second skill, do homework assignment B." She continually makes opportunities to talk with students individually, in small groups, and as a whole class about the quality of their decision making.

High quality middle level curriculum reveals and encourages a variety of talents in a variety of learners. Adolescents tend to describe themselves in terms of what they can do. This is both a blessing and a curse for teachers. It is helpful for students during this rocky period of development to be aware of their strengths. On the other hand, it's also critical that they realize ability is dynamic rather than static and that their investment in the work of learning will positively enhance the abilities they know they have as well as enable them to develop other abilities they don't yet see in themselves. Their teachers, then, need to affirm their evident strengths and push them to discover and develop other areas. Effective middle level curriculum will provide students opportunities to tap into, expose, and develop an expanding array of abilities.

Mr. Craft helps his students discover many ways that history is revealed and communicated. When students have important culminating projects to do, he makes sure there are multiple ways for them to express their learning. He models options for them and creates product cards that contain descriptors of quality work in different formats (for example, political cartoons, debates, Podcasts, monologues, and symposia). He also invites students to suggest modes of expressing key knowledge, understandings, and skills and to develop product cards for those forms that other students can use to guide their work later. In recent months, for example, he has had student proposals that included a short rock musical about the American Revolution, a public service campaign to raise awareness of the price our ancestors have paid for our freedoms, and a series of monologues based on letters from Civil War soldiers and diaries of slaves during the same era. In each instance, students were responsible for incorporating the knowledge, understandings, and skills from the state standards and district curriculum.

High quality middle level curriculum responds to the unique needs of highly able students. Just as it is important for teachers to understand key affective needs of bright middle level learners and to address those needs through learning environments that are positive and productive for them, it is also important that teachers of high-performing and high potential middle schoolers understand and attend to their cognitive needs through curriculum that is positive and productive for these learners.

In some ways, learning is like intellectual weight lifting. Physically speaking, if students are consistently asked to train with weights that are beyond their capacity to lift, those students do not develop muscles; rather, they learn to fear or dislike weight lifting, risk or actually experience injury, and, consequently, disengage from weight training as often as possible and through whatever means possible. Similarly, if students are consistently asked to "lift *intellectual* weights" that are well beyond their mental readiness to do so, rather than developing "intellectual muscles," they are likely to disengage from the learning process. This is often the plight of students who, for a variety of reasons, are given schoolwork that is beyond their current readiness with inadequate support to build the readiness.

Conversely, if students are asked to physically lift weights that are too light for them, they also fail to develop muscle; rather, they find the process of weight lifting to be tedious and pointless and often check out of the exercise regimen altogether. To continue the analogy, students who are advanced intellectually do not develop their capacities when the "intellectual weights" they are asked to lift in the classroom are too light for them. Like all other students, these middle schoolers need intellectual weight lifting that pushes them a bit beyond their current capacities and supports them in wrestling with tasks that extend them to a new level of intellectual strength. It is as frustrating and counterproductive for advanced learners to "practice" what they already know how to do as it is for struggling learners to "practice" what they currently have no hope of doing.

High quality middle level curriculum for very bright middle schoolers causes them to think more deeply, more broadly, more originally, and more critically than they already do. Certainly, curriculum that is concept based promotes the skills of empowerment, offers choice, is highly relevant to individuals, develops a wide range of talents, and forms a solid foundation for providing intellectual challenge for very bright middle level learners. In Chapter 4, we'll look more closely at what it means and does not mean to extend challenge beyond even that foundation for students who need to lift larger weights to continue developing intellectually. Chapter 5 will then explore some instructional strategies that are useful in providing challenge for highly able learners at the middle level.

The chart that follows (Figure 6) suggests some intellectual characteristics of highly able middle schoolers to which effective curriculum will respond. The chart is not exhaustive in its listing of traits, and it is not the case that every bright middle schooler exhibits all of the traits all of the time or in all subjects. Nonetheless, the traits are common among very bright middle school students and can help us understand ways in which curriculum can serve these students most appropriately. Note that not all of the traits are "positive." Like all students, bright kids have rough spots that need attention.

Figure 6

Sample Key Traits of Bright Middle Schoolers	Some Needs Suggested by the Traits	Some Ways Curriculum Can Appropriately Address the Traits
Rapid Learning	— To learn at a pace that is brisk for that student.	— Allow students to read ahead. — Provide an option for early tests of proficiency. — Ensure that work is appropriately challenging so that bright students can't work through it too quickly.
High Curiosity	— To raise and find answers to personally interesting questions.	— Make time for students to raise and pursue questions. — Provide opportunity for students to carry out independent study. — Encourage students to select supplementary reading of personal interest. — Use inquiry-based approaches to teaching and learning.

continued

FIGURE 6

Sample Key Traits of Bright Middle Schoolers	Some Needs Suggested by the Traits	Some Ways Curriculum Can Appropriately Address the Traits
Impatience	— To learn to tolerate ambiguity. — To learn persistence in the face of challenge. — To learn appreciation for the experiences of others.	— Ensure that work is complex enough to require persistence. — Necessitate that students find multiple approaches to solving a problem rather than one "right" or "best" way. — Commend the importance of each person's challenging himself or herself and celebrate any student having done so. — Set personal and whole-class goals for students (and have them do so).
Ability to Think in Abstract and Complex Ways— Sensitivity to Meaning	— To grapple with advanced questions and issues. — To use advanced resources. — To probe issues such as fairness, justice, or reasons for decisions.	— Provide versions of tasks that require use of advanced and primary resources and consultation with experts. — Use reflective journals to probe meaning. — Pose complex questions in class and encourage students to do so. — Make sure very bright students have regular opportunities to work with peers at a similar thinking and reasoning level. — Use simulations, authentic tasks, real-world products.
Passionate About Topics of Personal Interest	— To pursue those topics at an advanced level in ways that connect with school— "permission" to work on what matters most. — Recognition that some very bright middle schoolers also change passions often.	— Use independent studies, Webquests, Web inquiry. — Support students in developing products that incorporate essential learning goals while allowing exploration of student interests. — Allow students to demonstrate mastery early and use remaining time to work on areas of personal passion. — Use expert groups based on student interest as a teaching tool. — Support short-term, in-depth exploration of topics and ideas that interest students. — Talk with students about their interests as often as possible.

FIGURE 6

Sample Key Traits of Bright Middle Schoolers	Some Needs Suggested by the Traits	Some Ways Curriculum Can Appropriately Address the Traits
Stubborn About Opinions	— To look at issues from varied perspectives, develop open-mindedness, see shades of grey rather than only black and white, tolerate ambiguity, find more satisfaction in digging deeper than in being right.	— Create tasks that require students to explore multiple solutions, take on multiple roles, look at issues from unfamiliar vantage points, present convincing arguments other than their own, argue the efficacy of several solutions, consult experts who see issues differently than they do.
Intellectually Playful	— To play with words, ideas, humor, connections.	— Allow role playing. — Give assignment options such as cartoons and parodies. — Encourage students to study people who use humor successfully and determine characteristics of successful, respectful humor. — Use examples of student humor to enliven class. — Use brainstorming, metaphorical or analogical thinking, and "what if" questions. — Value creative thinking by modeling it, showing examples of it, and including it in rubrics and checklists for quality work.

Students who have high potential but are not high achievers are likely to have many of the same traits as their high-achieving peers. The traits are sometimes less obvious, displayed in a more challenging way, or perhaps even intentionally hidden. Nonetheless, they are there; and an observant teacher who is looking for the potential in every student will notice the clever approach to a problem, a surprising question, or a bit of sophisticated humor. It is very important to "teach up" to these students rather than "teaching down." In other words, teachers should not let less than stellar performance establish low ceilings of expectation for the student. It will serve the student far better for the teacher to provide both challenging tasks and the support (both academic and affective) to ensure student success in, or at least substantial growth toward, meeting the challenge.

For many high potential middle level learners, the door to academic success hinges on a teacher who is willing to establish a relationship of trust and respect with the student and simultaneously invite the student into a world where knowledge is dynamic, relevant, and purposeful. All this should be done while mentoring, coaching, and supporting the student's success in a new arena. It is likely that a key reason we have not been successful in tapping the possibilities of many high potential students who don't perform well in school is that we have not understood and invested deeply in that combination.

In Chapter 4, we'll look at some ways of thinking about and providing challenge for high-performing and high potential middle level learners. The success of the ideas and approaches will be rooted in positive classroom affect, environment, and powerful curriculum. ❖

Learn More About Quality Curriculum, Quality Curriculum in the Middle Grades, and Quality Curriculum for High Ability Learners

Beane, J. (1997). *Curriculum integration: Designing the core of democratic education.* New York: Teachers College Press.

Brandt, R. (1998). *Powerful learning.* Alexandria, VA: Association for Supervision and Curriculum Development.

Costa, A., & Kallick, B. (2000). *Discovering and exploring habits of mind.* Alexandria, VA: Association for Supervision and Curriculum Development.

Erickson, H. (2006). *Concept-based curriculum for the thinking classroom.* Thousand Oaks, CA: Corwin Press.

Jackson, A., & Davis, G. (2002). *Turning points 2000: Educating adolescents in the 21st century.* New York: Teachers College Press.

National Middle School Association (2003). *This we believe: Developmentally responsive middle level schools.* Westerville, OH: Author.

Springer, M. (1994). *Watershed: A successful voyage into integrative learning.* Columbus, OH: National Middle School Association.

Tomlinson, C., & McTighe, J. (2006). *Integrating differentiated instruction and understanding by design: Connecting kids and content.* Alexandria, VA: Association for Supervision and Curriculum Development.

VanTassel-Baska, J. (2003). *Content-based curriculum for low income and minority gifted learners* (Research Monograph RM03180). Storrs, CT: National Research Center on the Gifted and Talented. University of Connecticut.

VanTassel-Baska, J., & Little, C. (Eds.). (2003). *Content-based curriculum for high-ability learners.* Waco, TX: Prufrock.

Wiggins, G., & McTighe, J. (1998). *Understanding by design.* Alexandria, VA: Association for Supervision and Curriculum Development.

4

Extending the Challenge
of Quality Curriculum

*I now have a whole new view of poetry. When I used to read
poetry, I was in Boresville. I hated it, so I was very unhappy
to know that we were going to have to write it. I came into the
first poem we had to write with a lot of anger, until I suddenly
realized that I had gotten all my feelings out by writing! I
felt ten times better because I wasn't holding my emotions in
anymore. I was writing from my heart.... I felt like jumping
inside because I had finally done something well. I was proud.*

—Louie, 7th Grade

*If it's okay with you, could you please not grade my writing any
more? Every paper we've been assigned, I wrote at the breakfast
table the day it was due, or else on the bus on the way to
school. On every one of them, you gave me an "A," and that's
not what an "A" should be for.*

—Heather, 8th Grade

Louie was a middle schooler with high potential and generally low performance. He saw himself as alienated from school and from achievement. That's how others saw him. The experience with poetry that he described helped him see himself quite differently. The experience began with a teacher who chose to look past what he was doing to what he could do. She talked with him in ways that reflected a highly positive image of him. She planned curriculum to connect with where he was and designed experiences to transport him to where he needed to be. She read to the students poetry she loved and poetry she wrote. She also read them poems representing the ethnicities in their class. Perhaps most importantly, she introduced them to poets who experienced the feelings they knew in their lives—and helped them articulate those feelings in ways that were both satisfying and safe. In that context, she used expert language to talk about poetry and expected the students to do the same.

In other words, the teacher made certain that she connected with Louie and his classmates affectively. She developed an environment that was highly positive. She created curriculum that was authentic, meaning-rich, and personally relevant and recognized the need of young adolescents to look inward and outward in what they study.

Challenge for bright middle schoolers is rooted in those characteristics. Said another way, there's no such thing as quality learning for very bright middle schoolers that isn't first quality learning for all middle schoolers.

> *There's no such thing as quality learning for very bright middle schoolers that isn't first quality learning for all middle schoolers.*

In every middle school there are highly able students who are literally starving for challenge that extends even beyond what constitutes quality curriculum and instruction in general. That was Heather's dilemma. The work in her classes was quite challenging for many of her agemates, but it was under-challenging for her. She wanted to be recognized for something that indicated real achievement for her. The As she was getting felt dishonest to her; and, in fact, they were. They did not indicate that she was performing at a level of personal excellence, but rather that, in terms of what teachers expected of students with less academic talent, she was doing well.

This chapter offers some ways of thinking about what it means to provide that sort of challenge and to explore the role of the teacher in helping bright students succeed at new levels of challenge—beyond that provided even by quality curriculum. Planning for advanced level challenge for advanced level students is challenging for teachers, too. It's something that we, as teachers, have to learn to do. The good news is that as we learn, we become better teachers of bright kids and of most other students as well.

Planning for Challenge

Experts in the field of gifted education have proposed a number of ways of envisioning advanced level challenge. Each of them has the goal of extending the academic capacities of students who either already perform beyond expectations or could do so. Coaches of talented athletes work consistently to develop the abilities of those athletes, and they understand that doing so will call on them to provide exercises, drills, and responsibilities that are beyond the readiness of many others on the team. Teachers of talented musicians routinely provide extremely talented musicians with more advanced scores, call on them to understand the music more deeply and interpret it more subtly, and generally hold them to a higher standard of performance than would be appropriate for many other musicians of a similar age. Teaching students with great academic talent is no different. It's our role to be talent scouts and talent developers. We, too, need to prepare ourselves to work with students who may know more than we do about a subject, who may learn faster than we're accustomed to, who may question more deeply than is comfortable for us, *and* who are, of course, young adolescents with all the complexities that entails. Thinking about what challenge is and is not is a good place to start.

What challenge is not

A key principle of providing appropriate challenge for bright learners is that learning experiences for these students should differ in complexity, *not* quantity. It's not helpful to do more math problems that you already know how to solve, or to write more book reports, or answer more questions at the end of the chapter than other students. In other words, avoid *more* as a way of thinking about challenge.

Further, challenge should not seem punitive to students. Challenging work will not call on advanced learners to do two hours of science homework while other students complete their work in one hour. It will not be presented in a way that suggests to students the teacher is out to prove the student is not so smart, after all. Rather, challenging work helps students see the purpose in challenge and helps them understand that they are extending their own possibilities as a result of it.

Finally, challenging work will not be hopelessly beyond the capacity of the students asked to complete it. All learners—including those who are very advanced academically—grow when tasks are a little too difficult for them and when there is a support system that helps them succeed with the task. Returning to our weight training analogy, students' intellectual muscles grow only when they are presented with intellectual weight lifting tasks that require a bit of stretch, sweat, and strain—and the occasional assistance of a more capable "spotter."

> *All learners—including those who are very advanced academically—grow when tasks are a little too difficult for them and when there is a support system that helps them succeed with the task.*

General guidelines for developing challenge

There are some generic or general approaches to creating challenging work for highly able learners that have served these learners and their teachers well for a long time. Consider the options that follow.

Use advanced resources. You might bookmark more advanced Web sites for use by bright learners in research, provide college level texts as supplementary materials in class, encourage students to read adult level biographies about adults in fields of interest to them, consult newspapers such as the *New York Times* or *Wall Street Journal* when working with current events, and investigate primary sources. This is a reasonably simple way to provide challenge. because advanced sources employ advanced vocabulary, sentence structures, ideas, and viewpoints which can be very satisfying to students whose knowledge, understandings, and skills are beyond grade-level expectations.

Move from facts to meaning. Many advanced middle level learners are ready to infer principles in science, literature, and history. They are eager to seek out the significance of decisions. They are ready to generalize across topics within a subject and across subjects. They are ready to deal with multiple and even conflicting meanings related to a topic or issue. Focusing their work on meaning rather than "just the facts" is likely to be both more rewarding and more challenging.

Involve multiple concepts in a study. It may be that all seventh graders will examine the concept of "voice" in a literature unit. Students who are advanced in their understanding of voice in literature might examine how voice, diction, tone, setting, and mood interrelate.

Use multiple unknowns. Many students in math or science may be solving problems to find single unknowns. More advanced learners might benefit from working with problems with two or three unknowns.

Call on multiple skills. In a math class, students might apply knowledge about perimeter and area through construction and building tasks. Students with advanced knowledge about perimeter and area may design a doghouse for their middle school's mascot, the Huskie. Instructions for the doghouse may be written in a way that requires students to use area, perimeter, percentages, fractions, and simple questions.

Prompt student reflection. It is important that students develop increasing awareness of what lies behind their work—how they are thinking, planning, evaluating quality of work, sorting out ideas, making comparisons, changing as they learn, and so on. Advanced learners often have the capacity to do this sort of systematic thinking in the middle grades, yet they often do not. One reason for the discrepancy might well be that teachers don't require this sort of thinking from them and guide this sort of thinking in them. Because bright students often "shoot from the hip" with their thinking (and their work, in general), it's very important that they develop habits of reflectivity rather than impulsivity.

Study in depth or breadth. Students with a strong interest or talent in a particular area can feel very dissatisfied with the amount of information and insight presented in that area by typical school resources. When teachers provide time, opportunity, and appropriate structure to support students in learning much more about their areas of interest, the work is far more likely to challenge them than when they are limited to more cursory coverage of topics. Students might look at the people behind a topic or issue, how the topic or issue has evolved over time, how experts work with it, how the topic or issue plays out in different locations, how it is likely to change in the future, who the topic or issue affects, and so on.

Make unexpected connections. Bright middle schoolers often seek out connections among topics and ideas. School can seem segmented to them if it doesn't promote making connections. Teachers might ask advanced learners and creative learners to make metaphors to explain ideas; to develop analogies between topics, subjects, or ideas; to develop principles or generalizations that cut across topics or subjects and demonstrate their connectedness; to look at how events in history affect science and vice versa; to make connections between ideas in class and what's taking place in the world or in their own lives; or to examine how seemingly random events impact the development of a topic or issue.

Vary the pace. Often, highly able learners can and should learn required knowledge and skills more rapidly than many agemates. When it is possible for students to learn math more quickly or complete a book more quickly, it is wise to allow them to do that so that they can move on with their learning. We often call this "acceleration." It's important to remember that for the student who needs to move ahead, the pace is not "accelerated" or "fast." For that student, it's a normal or comfortable pace. At other times, a highly able student may want to work on a task or project longer than other agemates to allow for broader or deeper investigations. For many bright students, this is quite feasible. They may be able to substitute the broader work for homework or class work they don't really need to do, to modify a project assignment to allow more time for deeper study, or to skip a segment of study that is not critically important or in which they are already proficient to keep learning about something of particular interest at a level that's challenging for them.

Look at issues and controversies related to the topic. Working with issues and controversies is likely to be challenging because there is seldom just one right answer. In such situations, students must examine topics from varied vantage points as well as draw from expert level information and resources. To make meaning of the topic, students are forced to live with ambiguity for a time, which helps students expand their thinking.

Make and support opposing positions and arguments. Because very bright kids are so often "right," they may begin to believe that their views and opinions are inviolate. They need to be challenged to consider perspectives other than their own and to represent multiple positions accurately and fervently. Even when highly able students don't have strong personal positions on a topic or issue, it's challenging for them to learn about and represent the varied ways of thinking from people who do!

Work like a professional. Advanced learners can also find considerable challenge when their teachers ask them to use professional-level vocabulary, consult professional level resources, deal with unsolved problems in the field, create the kinds of products professionals in a field use to share their findings, develop the habits of mind and thought that typify experts in an area, and engage in the learning and problem-solving processes an expert would use.

Models for Developing Challenge

Next, we'll take a look at three specific models for developing challenge. The models are designed to stretch the capacities of high-performing and high potential learners—including those in the middle grades—in the context of positive classroom environments and quality curriculum.

Kaplan's model for developing advanced challenge

A longtime contributor to understanding the learning needs of highly able students and providing appropriate academic challenge for them, Sandra Kaplan (1994) suggested a five-pronged approach to stretching the capacities of bright learners. The model is very well suited to the

developing capacities of middle level learners. The chart that follows
(Figure 7) provides the model's elements and briefly describes ways in
which teachers can incorporate the components into curriculum. You
will notice overlap with the general strategies presented in the previous
section of the chapter, but the model provides additional explanations and
applications of the various elements and proposes additional elements.
Kaplan also noted that it is important to have students work with the
elements simultaneously. A teacher could use the table in Figure 8 to
brainstorm ways of supporting both depth and complexity. For example,
a science teacher might develop a product assignment for all students, in
which they examine factors that influence a local ecosystem and actions
that might be taken to protect it. The teacher might extend the product
assignment for highly able science students by asking them to examine
how perspectives of citizens and government officials about the ecosystem
have changed over the last 50 years and how those changes might predict
future patterns in the health of the ecosystem. This modification was
derived by asking students to relate different perspectives, over time, in
regard to trends and patterns (note the shaded boxes in Figure 8).

FIGURE 7

Elements of Kaplan's Model	Explanation of the Elements	Ways to Apply the Elements in Curriculum Design
Pace	— Accelerating the rate at which a student develops and demonstrates mastery.	
Depth	— Exploring the details, patterns, rules, ethics, and unanswered questions of a discipline.	— Move from the familiar to the unfamiliar, from concrete to abstract, from known to unknown. — Move beyond facts to examine the concepts, principles, theories, and laws that undergird the disciplines. — Ask students to layer their study by looking at details, patterns, unanswered questions, trends, and ethical considerations of a topic or discipline.

FIGURE 7

Elements of Kaplan's Model	Explanation of the Elements	Ways to Apply the Elements in Curriculum Design
Complexity	— Making connections over time, seeing relationships, looking at ideas within, across, and among disciplines.	— Study the themes, problems, and issues in a discipline. — Look for relationships among ideas within a topic, within a discipline, and across disciplines. Examine relationships in the past, present, and future. — Look at relationships from multiple perspectives (for example, looking at the Roaring '20s as a sociologist, psychologist, artist, historian, and musician).
Novelty	— Seeking original interpretations, challenging existing ideas, looking for new ways of expression and new uses of technologies, materials, or forms.	— Develop new ideas or approaches by looking from multiple perspectives, coming at the topic in a new way, or using a new way of thinking. — Communicate ideas, feelings, and conclusions using new methods and techniques.
Independence	— Promoting self-direction and the skills of self-directed learning.	— Build on student interest. — Have students select topics for extended study. — Help the student understand and develop appropriate methods for the study. — Allow a student the maximum reasonable freedom to design and pursue the study. — Provide support and structure to help the student grow in independence (for example: time lines, acquisition of reliable resources, data gathering and analysis, self-monitoring). — Ensure high standards of work and production.

FIGURE 8

		COMPLEXITY		
		Relate Over Time	Different Perspectives	Across Disciplines
D	Language of the discipline			
E	Details, facts of the topic or discipline			
P	Patterns in the discipline			
T	Rules of the discipline			
H	Trends in the discipline			
	Unanswered questions in the topic or discipline			
	Ethics of the discipline			
	Big ideas, principles of the topic or discipline			

The "Equalizer" as a way of thinking about challenge

Tomlinson's work (2001) on differentiated instruction—or instruction that is responsive to learners' varying needs—includes a mechanism for adjusting challenge so that it is appropriate for a particular learner or group of learners at a particular time. The Equalizer (Figure 9) is designed to look like the tuning mechanism on a CD player. We're accustomed to moving sliding buttons to the left or right on a tuner to adjust pitch, tone, volume, fade, and so on. Sometimes the sound is good without moving any of the buttons. At other times, we improve or refine the sound by moving one or two of the buttons. Seldom, if ever, do we slide all the buttons to the far left or far right. It's a matter of calibration.

Similarly, the Equalizer suggests that a teacher "fine tune" a task, assessment, or product by moving one or two of the buttons, and revising the assignment accordingly, so that the work extends the knowledge, understandings, or skills of a learner or group of learners by providing appropriate challenge. Remember that challenge is appropriate for a student when (a) the work is a little too hard for that student and (b) there is a support system to help the student reach the new level of performance required by the task.

FIGURE 9

The Equalizer

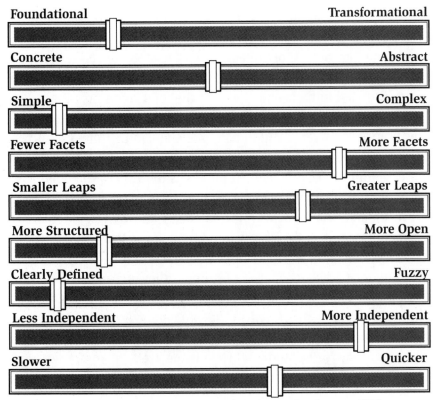

(Source; Association for Supervision and Curriculum Development, 2001)

The diagram shows nine continuums along which teachers can make adjustments to calibrate challenge for learner needs. Tasks can move from simple to complex, from single-faceted to multi-faceted, from requiring smaller mental leaps to greater mental leaps, from providing more structure (scaffolding) for a student to providing less, from clearly defined problems to ones that are fuzzier or less well defined, from requiring less independence on the part of the student to requiring a great deal of independence in completing the work, and from a slower pace to a quicker pace. In general, more advanced learners will be challenged by tasks closer to the right sides of the continuums. The words above a continuum suggest elements in curriculum or instruction that a teacher might adjust.

For example, a science teacher whose students are investigating how black holes work might use the third continuum of the Equalizer, providing students who are reading well below grade level with some research materials that are *simpler* in terms of vocabulary, sentence structure, and explanations. Simultaneously, he may provide research materials at a high school or college level of readability (more *complex* in terms of vocabulary, explanations, and sentence structure) for students who are advanced in their knowledge of the topic and in reading.

A social studies teacher is asking her students to read some newspaper articles from World War II and to compare and contrast them with some editorial cartoons from the same period. She will use the seventh continuum (*clearly defined* problems to *fuzzier* problems) as one way of thinking about "differentiating" the challenge level of the task. All students will work with the same key knowledge, essential understandings, and skills. However, one version of the task will contain step-by-step directions for the comparison and contrast task and a graphic organizer students can use as they gather information and draw conclusions. In other words, their "process" of work and thought will be quite scaffolded or *structured* so that students who need guidance in logical, step-by-step thinking will have that support. In essence, the directions will say to the student, "Here is the problem you're working on, and here are the steps you should follow in arriving at a solution to the problem."

The directions for students who are more comfortable with the "process" of reading, gathering information, and drawing conclusions from that information, however, will be *fuzzier.* For these students, instructions might say something like, "Here are some articles and political cartoons related to _____. Compare and contrast the articles with regard to discrepancies you believe are important in our understanding of the time period, and be ready to share your conclusions with the class." Here, students must identify the problems on their own, determine how to present them, and figure out the steps they will follow in the task. In other words, their task, including working *processes,* are less defined—therefore calling on students to manage the ambiguities and decision-making processes themselves.

Just as we might move two (or more) buttons on a CD tuner, the teacher might do so in planning with the Equalizer as well. For example, the social studies teacher might also provide a range of articles and cartoons from *simpler* to more *complex,* as well as providing a **structured problem** for students who need the structure and a *fuzzier* problem for others ready for the structure to "fall away."

The Equalizer suggests that all students need tasks that are appropriately challenging for them at a given time. Challenge is not absolute but relative to individuals and their growth. A teacher using the Equalizer would be attuned to ensuring that highly able students feel challenged by the day's work as well as ensuring appropriate challenge for a student who is struggling with a topic, or a skill. The Equalizer also helps us remember that student development is fluid. It "slides" along a continuum depending upon an array of factors. Teachers who try to guide students along the developmental continuums are more likely to foster persistent growth along those continuums—to structure tasks that progress *with* students— than are teachers who assume that there is "one size" of challenge that will stretch all students.

When a teacher adjusts the challenge level of a task, assessment, or product using the Equalizer, it is called "tiering." Many kinds of student work can be tiered—homework, learning centers, assessments, writing assignments, problems, labs, and others. The goal of tiering is always to ensure challenge for a student just above that student's comfort level so that the student is always working to grow, not working in frustration or marching in place.

> *The goal of tiering is always to ensure challenge for a student just above that student's comfort level so that the student is always working to grow, not working in frustration or marching in place.*

Ascending Intellectual Demand—A way of thinking about challenge

The Parallel Curriculum Model (PCM), developed by Carol Tomlinson, Sandra Kaplan, Joe Renzulli, Jeanne Purcell, Jann Leppien, and Deborah Burns (2002), also makes the point that all students should have access to and support in mastering high level curriculum that forces the students to reason in order to make authentic meaning of the disciplines. PCM suggests that teachers craft curriculum to engage students in four parallel ways of thinking about what they study: (1) identifying and understanding the *key knowledge, concepts, principles,* and *skills* of the discipline; (2) helping students see how the key concepts and principles help them *connect* knowledge within and across disciplines, time periods, and places; (3) use the key knowledge, concepts, principles, and skills to *work like practitioners* in the disciplines; and (4) use the key concepts and principles of the discipline to *reflect on their own lives,* experiences, and futures. PCM advocates that all students work in these four parallel ways (which incorporate, but aren't limited by required content standards) that the model calls the (1) Core Parallel, (2) Parallel of Connections, (3) Parallel of Practice, and (4) Parallel of Identity. The model is an excellent fit for the developmental needs of all middle level learners.

As a means of extending challenge for students who can move beyond even this rich and multifaceted approach, the Parallel Curriculum Model proposes "Ascending Intellectual Demand" or AID. AID is based on the premise that teachers can extend challenge for learners by asking them to work increasingly like experts in a field. In other words, continuing challenge stems from persistent movement toward expertise.

AID presents three mechanisms teachers can use to modify curriculum for advanced learners by guiding students toward expertise. First, teachers might simply review assignments, *looking for ways in which students might be asked to work that characterize the work of experts.* As teachers develop instructions and criteria for success that call on students to work in expert-like ways, it's likely that advanced learners will encounter appropriate challenge. Among the traits and skills of experts are

- Investing time in understanding the background and contexts of problems
- Engaging others in reflective conversations to gather data and solve problems
- Looking for many, relevant resources to aid understanding
- Gleaning pertinent information from seemingly extraneous data
- Posing insightful questions about content and ways of working
- Organizing knowledge to enhance meaning and usefulness
- Distinguishing differences between typical and novel examples
- Transferring knowledge and skills to unfamiliar contexts
- Seeking patterns in data
- Looking for alternative views and solutions beyond one's own
- Seeking useful connections among ideas
- Creating new and useful applications
- Developing effective and efficient systems for learning and problem solving
- Looking for significant ideas and events
- Reflecting on one's own thinking and its effectiveness in situations
- Looking for subtle examples and illustrations
- Working at high levels of abstract, analytical, and creative thinking
- Demonstrating high levels of curiosity
- Seeking deep understanding of a topic
- Raising questions about reasons for and use of knowledge
- Inspiring oneself to work hard
- Demonstrating commitment to excellence
- Seeking useful critique of one's work
- Looking for insights

- Using present knowledge to plan for future directions in work and learning
- Examining the impact of decisions on self, others, and society.

Adapted from Tomlinson, et al.(2006). *The Parallel Curriculum in the Classroom, Book I: Essays for Application Across the Content Areas, K–12*, p. 87. Corwin Press.

A second way of thinking about Ascending Intellectual Demand, or movement toward expertise, involves using a series of prompts in curriculum design that also focus student attention on ideas and ways of working that reflect expertise. There are four sets of prompts, each designed to help students think more deeply and work more like experts in regard to one of the four PCM "parallels" (Core, Connections, Practice, and Identity). In Figure 10 are samples of AID prompts for the parallels. Teachers can use these in designing classroom questions, journal prompts, tasks, assessments, and products for students.

FIGURE 10

Sample AID Prompts for Understanding and Applying Key Concepts and Principles at Increasingly Expert-Like Levels

- Call on students to use more advanced reading, resource, and research materials.
- Design tasks or products that are more open-ended or ambiguous in nature.
- Have students apply what they are learning to contexts very different from examples studied in class.
- Design tasks that prompt students to reflect on the significance of ideas and information.
- Call on students to generate new and useful ways to represent ideas and solutions.
- Include directions that call on students to establish criteria for high quality work, assess their progress according to those criteria, and seek feedback that improves their work and methods of working.

FIGURE 10

Sample AID Prompts for Using Key Concepts and Principles to Make Connections Within and Across Disciplines, Times, and Places

- Ask students to develop solutions, proposals, or approaches that bridge differences in perspectives and still effectively address a problem or issue.
- Develop tasks or products that cause students to look for patterns of interaction among multiple areas (for example, ways in which geography, economics, politics, and technology affect one another).
- Develop tasks and products that enclourage students to articulate unstated assumptions that lie beneath the surface of beliefs, discussions, approaches, and solutions.
- Call on students to look at broad segments of the world from perspectives quite different than their own (for example, how a teenager in an economically depressed country might view housing, clothing, gadgets, relationships with adults, plans for the future).

Sample AID Prompts for Working with Key Information, Concepts, Principles, and Skills Used by Practitioners in a Discipline

- Encourage students to distinguish between approaches to solving problems that seem authentic and relevant to the discipline and those that seem less authentic or less relevant.
- Call on students to use the language experts would use in reflecting on issues and problems in a discipline.
- Have students work on problems currently causing difficulty for experts in a discipline.
- Structure problems that will cause students to engage in persistent, prolonged work on a topic or problem, including engaging in persistent reflection about their own thinking and work.
- Call on students to compare and contrast their own approaches to discipline-based work with those of experts in the field.

Sample AID Prompts for Using Key Concepts and Principles to Reflect on One's Own Life and Experiences

- Ask students to collaborate with an expert in a discipline and reflect on what that experience reveals to students about their own interests, beliefs, and ways of working.
- Have the students look for biases, blind spots, and assumptions that typify the field; compare those with their own.
- Ask students to find and reflect on the meaning of paradoxes in the field and to do the same with paradoxes in their lives.
- Conduct an ethnographic study of a facet of the field and reflect on both findings and personal revelations.
- Examine key concepts in a discipline (e.g., conflict, scarcity, power) and in one's own life; reflect on how understanding one application informs the other.

A third way of thinking about Ascending Intellectual Demand or movement toward expertise guides teachers in thinking about *how experts develop over time and where particular students are in that journey* of development in regard to a particular discipline at a particular time. Working with the PCM authors, Kelly Hedrick developed a series of six charts to help teachers understand the progression toward expertise. The first graphic, "Novice to Expert Continuum" (Figure 11, p. 77) suggests characteristics of novices, apprentices, practitioners, and experts. She reminds us of the important truth that expertise develops in terms of one's knowledge, skills, attitudes, and habits of mind. A very bright sixth grader, for instance, may look like a practitioner in his knowledge about math; but that same student might be largely a novice in his work habits. The arrows at the bottom of each graphic also remind us that the journey toward expertise is more like an ebb and flow rather than a linear path. That is, a student may look much like an expert in creating and using maps, but become a novice again when encountering three-dimensional maps.

The second graphic, "Teacher Response to Student Development of Expertise" (Figure 12), takes us to an important next step and suggests specific ways a teacher might support challenge and growth for students at various stages of the journey toward expertise. For example, a language arts teacher who is working with all students on autobiographical writing might provide novice writers who are still struggling with annotated writing samples of effective opening paragraphs and checklists of important components in autobiographies and might meet often with a small group of such writers to provide guided practice on key elements of this form of writing. For students who are much more proficient writers (perhaps at a practitioner level), the teacher might conduct small-group conversations where students examine one another's writing as well as that of professional biographers and work with open inquiry about various approaches to developing compelling autobiographical prose.

The final four graphics (Figures 13-16) provide a critical final step in helping us understand how experts might "look" as they develop in science, history, language arts/English, and mathematics. If we use the guides to examine student work, we can (1) see the range of development in our classes, (2) recognize traits of individuals, and (3) draw on the descriptors to develop curriculum that serves as a catalyst for the growth of students in knowledge, skills, attitudes, and habits of mind wherever they are on the continuum in our subject area.

Summary Thoughts About Challenge

The guides for thinking about challenge for high ability and high potential learners presented in this chapter make several assumptions:

1. **All students need and deserve consistent challenge in their classes.**
2. **Challenge is personal—that is, what challenges one student may not challenge another.**
3. **Even for an individual, what constitutes challenge will change as contexts change.**
4. **Teachers can plan for challenge by studying their students and developing a growing sense of how to evoke and support escalating challenge.**

The models for developing challenge have many shared elements. That is because they each seek to respond to traits and needs common to many highly able learners. Drawing on elements common across the models (for example, focusing on concepts and principles, adjusting pace, studying in depth and breadth) are good first steps for teachers who seek to design curriculum that is responsive both to content requirements of states and districts and the highly able students they teach.

Two middle level teachers who work persistently to ensure advanced challenge for their advanced learners summed up their thinking on the topic. One seventh grade English teacher said about her highly able students, "Don't over teach them, don't over explain to them, don't over discipline them." The eighth grade math teacher advised, "Keep them running into a good, strong wind. Don't let them stand still too long. Coach them for the race. Then stand on the sidelines and cheer like crazy!" ❖

Learn More About Challenge for High Ability Learners

Kaplan, S. (1994). *Differentiating core curriculum and instruction to provide advanced learning opportunities.* Sacramento, CA: California Association for the Gifted.

Tomlinson, C. (1999). *The differentiated classroom: Responding to the needs of all learners.* Alexandria, VA: Association for Supervision and Curriculum Development.

Tomlinson, C. (2001). *How to differentiate instruction in mixed-ability classrooms* (2nd ed.). Alexandria, VA: Association for Supervision and Curriculum Development.

Tomlinson, C., Kaplan, S., Renzulli, J., Purcell, J., Leppien, J., & Burns, D. (2002). *The Parallel Curriculum Model: A design to develop high potential and challenge high ability learners.* Thousand Oaks, CA: Corwin Press.

Tomlinson, C., Kaplan, S., Purcell, J., Leppien, J., Burns, D., & Strickland, C. (2006). *The Parallel Curriculum in the classroom, Book I: Essays for application across the content areas, K–12.* Thousand Oaks, CA: Corwin Press.

Figure 11
"Novice to Expert Continuum"

Adapted from Tomlinson, et al.(2006). *The Parallel Curriculum in the Classroom, Book I: Essays for Application Across the Content Areas, K–12.* Corwin Press.

Ascending Intellectual Demand

Novice
- Experiences content at a concrete level
- Manipulates microconcepts one at a time
- Needs skill instruction and guided practice
- Requires support, encouragement, and guidance
- Seeks affirmation of competency to complete a task.

Apprentice
- Understands the connections among microconcepts within a discipline
- Connects information within a microconcept
- Begins to interpret generalizations and themes that connect concepts
- Applies skills with limited supervision
- Seeks confirmation at the end of a task
- Reflects upon content and skills when prompted.

Practitioner
- Manipulates two or more microconcepts simultaneously
- Creates generalizations that explain connections among concepts
- Selects and uses skills in order to complete a task
- Seeks input from others as needed
- Exhibits task commitment and persistence when challenges are moderate
- Reflects upon both content and skills to improve understanding and performance.

Expert
- Uses concepts within and among disciplines to derive theories and principles
- Creates innovations within a field
- Practices skill development independently and for the purpose of improvement
- Seeks input from other experts in a field for a specific purpose
- Works to achieve flow and derives pleasure from the experience (high challenge, and advanced skill or knowledge)
- Independent and self-directed learner
- Seeks experiences that cause a return to previous levels in varying degrees.

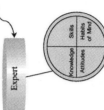

Novice — Apprentice — Practitioner — Expert (Knowledge, Skills, Attitudes, Habits of Mind)

78

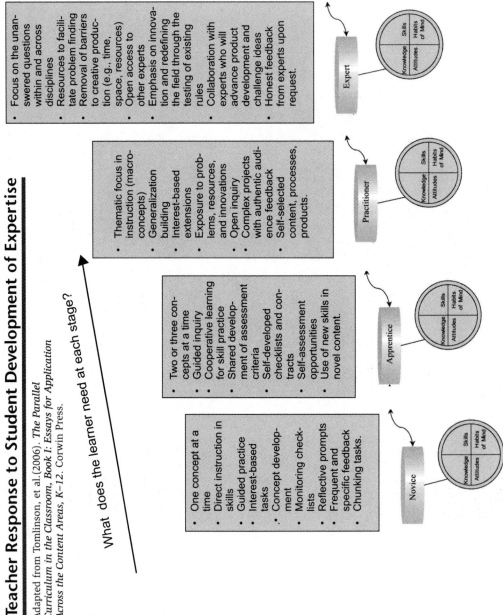

FIGURE 12

Teacher Response to Student Development of Expertise

Adapted from Tomlinson, et al. (2006). *The Parallel Curriculum in the Classroom, Book I: Essays for Application Across the Content Areas, K–12.* Corwin Press.

What does the learner need at each stage?

- Focus on the unanswered questions within and across disciplines
- Resources to facilitate problem finding
- Removal of barriers to creative production (e.g., time, space, resources)
- Open access to other experts
- Emphasis on innovation and redefining the field through the testing of existing rules
- Collaboration with experts who will advance product development and challenge ideas
- Honest feedback from experts upon request.

Expert

- Thematic focus in instruction (macro-concepts)
- Generalization building
- Interest-based extensions
- Exposure to problems, resources, and innovations
- Open inquiry
- Complex projects with authentic audience feedback
- Self-selected content, processes, products.

Practitioner

- Two or three concepts at a time
- Guided inquiry
- Cooperative learning for skill practice
- Shared development of assessment criteria
- Self-developed checklists and contracts
- Self-assessment opportunities
- Use of new skills in novel content.

Apprentice

- One concept at a time
- Direct instruction in skills
- Guided practice
- Interest-based tasks
- Concept development
- Monitoring checklists
- Reflective prompts
- Frequent and specific feedback
- Chunking tasks.

Novice

Skills | Habits of Mind
Knowledge | Attitudes

FIGURE 13

Expertise in
English Language Arts

Reference: *NCTE/IRA Standards for English Language Arts.*
Adapted from Tomlinson, et al.(2006). *The Parallel
Curriculum in the Classroom, Book I: Essays for Application
Across the Content Areas, K–12.* Corwin Press.

Novice

- Applies a limited range of skills in an algorithmic manner
- Understands the skills and concepts in isolation, but lacks flexibility in understanding and application
- Practices and applies skills when prompted
- Limits reading selections and resources to a narrow scope
- Written and oral communication is technically correct but lacks variety and personal relevance
- Sees written and oral communication and research with limited possibilities
- Views editing and revisions as punitive and drudgery.

Novice

Apprentice

- Demonstrates flexibility in the use of skills and the understanding of concepts
- Understands the connections across written and oral communication, reading, and research
- Understands the need for a variety of selections in reading, writing, and research
- Understands the role of effective communication for a variety of purposes
- Adjusts communication modes according to purpose and audience
- Values the input of qualified reviewers in the editing and revision process.

Apprentice

Practitioner

- Applies the skills of language arts in other disciplines with relative ease
- Moves fluidly among the various modes and methodologies associated with language arts
- Appreciates the art of communication
- Conducts authentic research applying the skills of questioning, information gathering, data analysis, and synthesis
- Understands the necessity for multiple and varied resources in research
- Seeks the constructive criticism of knowledgeable persons across disciplines in developing a product
- Understands and respects the diversity of language across cultures.

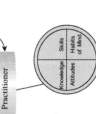
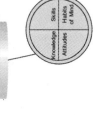

Practitioner

Expert

- Demonstrates knowledge, reflection, creativity and critical analysis of language arts skills and concepts across a wide variety of disciplines
- Applies the wide range of skills associated with effective oral and written communication, reading, and research with automaticity
- Reading, writing, speaking, and researching lead to personal fulfillment beyond the goals of learning and the exchange of information
- Appreciates the power of the written and spoken word
- Questions the accepted conventions and rules
- Experiments with methods to communicate and develop greater understanding
- Practices in all areas (i.e. written and oral communication, reading, and research).

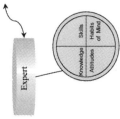

Expert

FIGURE 14
Expertise in
History

Reference: NCSS *Curriculum Standards for Social Studies*
Adapted from Tomlinson, et al. (2006). *The Parallel
Curriculum in the Classroom, Book I: Essays for Application
Across the Content Areas, K–12.* Corwin Press.

Novice

- Defines history as isolated people, places, and events
- Sees the facts and skills, but not the concepts that link them
- Studies history through rote memorization
- Needs experiences with sequencing to establish a sense of chronology
- Identifies causes and effects as isolated events
- Lacks an appreciation for history and its relevance to self and the world in the present and the future.

Apprentice

- Understands history at the conceptual level
- Seeks connections among microconcepts to make sense of historical patterns and trends
- Poses historical research questions
- Has a clearly defined sense of chronology
- Understands the complexity of causes and effects
- Recognizes the importance of perspective in historical events, human perspectives, and consequences.

Practitioner

- Analyzes contemporary events through an historical lens with automaticity
- Understands chronology, but has the ability to follow themes across events and time periods regardless of the direction (present to past, past to present)
- Identifies unanswered questions and crafts researchable questions to investigate them
- Understands the social, political, economic, and technological influences on patterns and trends
- Understands and appreciates the influence of individual experiences, societal values, and traditions on historical perspectives.

Expert

- Moves easily from the theoretical to the practical and vice versa in response to a situation
- Challenges accepted bodies of knowledge, methods, and research findings
- Develops themes and connections across historical events, periods, and fields without reliance, but acknowledgement of chronology
- Uses the knowledge and skills of the discipline across diverse fields and disciplines
- Displays curiosity and seeks challenge through unanswered questions in the field
- Marvels at the richness of history and its importance in shaping the present and future
- Systematically and with automaticity uses the knowledge, skills, and processes of the discipline to investigate.

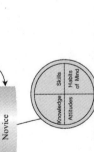

Novice

Apprentice

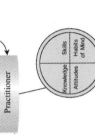

Practitioner

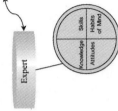

Expert

FIGURE 15

Expertise in

Mathematics

Reference: NCTM *Principles and Standards for School Mathematics*
Adapted from Tomlinson, et al. (2006). *The Parallel
Curriculum in the Classroom, Book I: Essays for Application
Across the Content Areas, K–12.* Corwin Press.

Novice

- Applies the skills of discrete mathematics, but lacks a conceptual understanding
- Identifies the principles, but cannot apply them unless prompted
- Computes efficiently, but lacks fluency
- Sees limited relationships among numbers and number systems
- Identifies only the most basic patterns
- Needs frequent feedback and assurance during problem solving
- Sees the "right answer" as the goal.

Apprentice

- Connects the relationships among mathematical facts and skills through concepts
- Computes fluently and makes reasonable estimates
- Applies skills with confidence and develops greater understanding beyond number and operations
- Makes connections across mathematical ideas
- Understands the principles that frame a field (i.e., measurement, algebra, geometry, statistics).

Practitioner

- Uses the principles of mathematics to make connections among concepts across multiple fields within mathematics
- Makes appropriate selections about which tools and methods to use
- Understands patterns, relations, and functions
- Applies skills with automaticity
- Understands change in a variety of contexts
- Uses a variety of tools and methods with efficiency in the analysis of mathematical situations
- Appreciates the role of mathematics in other disciplines
- Formulates questions for research that can be addressed through one or more fields of mathematics.

Expert

- Uses computation as merely a means to an end
- Questions existing mathematical principles
- Moves easily among the fields of mathematics through the use of macroconcepts
- Links mathematical principles to other fields through real-world problems
- Seeks the challenge of unresolved problems and the testing of existing theories
- Seeks flow through the manipulation of tools and methods in complex problem solving
- Views unanswered questions in other disciplines through the concepts of mathematics
- Uses reflection and practice as tools for self-improvement.

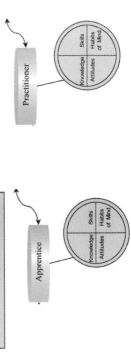

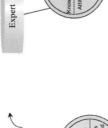

FIGURE 16
Expertise in
Science

Reference: *Benchmarks for Science Literacy.*
American Association for the Advancement of
Science Literacy: Project 2061.

Adapted from Tomlinson, et
al. (2006). *The Parallel Curriculum
in the Classroom, Book I: Essays
for Application Across the Content
Areas, K–12.* Corwin Press.

Novice

- Analyzes existing theories, principles, and rules
- Sees science as a body of facts and skills
- Seeks algorithmic tasks; ambiguity causes discomfort
- Experimentation is an end in itself rather than a means to an end
- Sees a disproved hypothesis as a failure
- Inadvertently includes and fails to manage multiple variables
- Science is isolated from other disciplines.

Novice

Apprentice

- Tests and manipulates existing theories, principles, and rules
- Sees science as a body of concepts and recognizes connections among the microconcepts
- Uses existing scientific questions for research and experimentation
- Tolerates the ambiguous nature of science
- Manipulates one variable within an experiment with ease
- Understands, identifies, and analyzes the relationships among the independent and dependent variables, constants, and controls
- Uses mathematics to conduct scientific work.

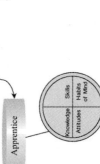

Apprentice

Practitioner

- Challenges existing theories, principles, and rules through research and experimentation
- Understands and appreciates that scientific knowledge is never declared certain
- Poses new scientific questions
- Operates comfortably in the ambiguity that characterizes science
- Effectively manipulates multiple variables within an experiment
- Plans for and observes a wide range of factors (variables, constants, controls) and discerns patterns
- Uses mathematics as the language of science.

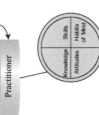

Practitioner

Expert

- Makes a contribution to the discipline or field (e.g., new experiments, new observations, new methods and tools, new theories, principles, and rules)
- Poses original scientific questions that test the limits of the existing body of knowledge
- Understands and assesses the relationships among the fields of science and other fields across multiple disciplines.
- Seeks and derives satisfaction from the ambiguous situations in science
- Conducts complex experiments with ease and fluidity; freely manipulates methods, tools, knowledge, and self to achieve desired results.

Expert

5

Instructional Strategies for Teaching High Ability and High Potential Learners

The thing about this class is that I can't slide in here. There's something new happening all the time. Our teacher keeps finding new ways to teach us. And the things she asks us to do ... well, you have to stay alert and think and give it your best. And we don't mind working in here because it doesn't so much feel like work. But it is, you know.

—Jason, 7th Grade

Safe and nourishing learning environments provide the setting in which highly able middle level learners can balance the dual gravities of achieving and belonging. Powerful curriculum provides the catalyst for bright middle schoolers to understand and develop their talents and interests while seeing beyond them to a deeper understanding of the disciplines they study. Personalized challenge provides the impetus and support that bright middle schoolers need to extend their abilities. Dynamic instruction provides the vehicle that transports bright middle schoolers through the terrain of personally challenging curriculum.

Instructional strategies effective in challenging high-performing and high potential learners must align with curriculum goals. They must also be appropriate in addressing the developmental needs of young adolescents and those of highly able young adolescents. The fields of middle level education and gifted education are in general agreement that appropriate instructional strategies in the middle grades should

- Be student centered
- Be socially oriented and interactive
- Be attentive to attention span needs of students
- Require disciplined inquiry
- Support curiosity
- Help students construct knowledge
- Promote students' growing independence
- Allow for choice
- Support students in developing meaningful products
- Be responsive to student diversity.

There is no instructional strategy we know of that "belongs" to high ability learners; rather, high quality instructional approaches benefit a very wide range of learners. Personally challenging curriculum delivered through dynamic instructional strategies is critical for the growth of all learners. The trick with high-end learners is to avoid the assumption that what constitutes challenge for students working at grade level will be challenging for students with very advanced performance.

> *No instructional strategy "belongs" to high ability learners; rather, high quality instructional approaches benefit a very wide range of learners.*

The remainder of this chapter will provide just a few examples of instructional strategies that: (1) are developmentally appropriate for middle school learners, (2) address the particular needs of highly able young adolescents, and (3) have strong potential to support the goals of high quality curriculum. In each instance, we'll describe the strategy, note why it is useful for young adolescents, and examine special considerations for use with very bright middle schoolers. Chapter 6 will provide scenarios of the strategies at work with some of the students introduced in Chapter 1.

Strategy One—Pre-assessment and Ongoing Assessment

Pre-assessment and ongoing assessment are not so much instructional strategies as they are the lifeline of informed teaching. Therefore, it is important for teachers to think of assessment with every iteration of instructional planning.

At the beginning of a year, it is really important for teachers to get a sense of each student's status with precursor skills. Who can read the textbook effectively, and who cannot? Who has the background vocabulary the teacher might assume will be in place, and who does not? Who mastered key skills from previous classes, and who did not? Teacher-developed instruments that provide at least a starting point for understanding a student's preparedness for next steps is crucial to teaching students rather than only covering content. In addition, it's very helpful at the beginning of the year to find out about students' current interests and preferred ways of learning. Teachers can get a sense of these factors through surveys, open-ended questions, student letters to teachers, and brief subject area autobiographies.

Similarly, at the outset of each unit of study, a teacher can gain incredibly valuable insights by pre-assessing students' knowledge, understandings, and skills related to that unit. Students with huge gaps in prior learning will need help in "patching potholes" before they can confidently move ahead. And it is of virtually no use to "teach" a student something he or she already knows.

> *It is of virtually no use to "teach" a student something he or she already knows.*

As each unit of study progresses, the most effective teachers continually ask themselves, *What are the essential goals for this unit and this lesson? How can I know how each student is progressing toward those goals? What can I do with that information in order to ensure each student's growth?* Ongoing assessment provides the answer to the second of those questions.

Ongoing assessment can be informal or formal. Teachers can help students learn to diagnose their own status on important goals and assign work that meets current needs. Teachers can use exit cards, quick quizzes, or journal entries to gain insight into student progress.

FIGURE 17

Sample Exit Card

Name: _____

3 most important things you learned about weather systems:

2 questions you still have or points that remain unclear:

1 aspect of weather systems you'd like to learn more about:

The exit card above (Figure 17) can open the lids of students' brains so that their teacher can peer inside to discover which material they've mastered, which aspects they're struggling with, and—of particular import for bright adolescents—which issues they'd like to explore in more depth. Homework, class work, and labs are other sources of ongoing assessment data. The goal of ongoing assessment is not to fill the grade book but rather to inform instruction. Hilda Taba has wisely counseled us that teaching in the dark is likely to be both inefficient and ineffective.

The inevitable range of learner variance during early adolescence combined with the variable rate of growth in students of this age make it highly unlikely that they will develop academically as they should when they are taught as though they are all essentially the same. To teach each student in this diverse population as he or she needs to be taught, teachers must have a clear sense of direction for a learning journey, must continually monitor where each student is along that route, and must adjust instruction as needed to ensure that every learner stays on course. Pre-assessment and ongoing assessment are simply non-negotiables for student success.

Very bright middle schoolers are simply part of the diversity in middle grades classrooms. They, like all other students, need to grow from their starting points. When pre-assessments reveal to teachers that students are already proficient with content the teacher has not yet taught, that's a signal to provide learning experiences beyond the "planned" curriculum that will enable these students to continue developing in their knowledge, attitudes about learning, and habits of mind and work. When ongoing assessments reveal that some students have mastered content while others have not, it is as important to plan for those students who are ready to move ahead as it is to plan for those who need additional instruction, practice, or support.

> *It is as important to plan for those students who are ready to move ahead as it is to plan for those who need additional instruction or support.*

Strategy Two—Think-Pair-Share

In this quick strategy, the teacher poses a "thought" question to the class. The question should help students begin to consider an essential idea or understanding for a lesson or unit or begin to explore an issue or problem the lesson or unit will confront. The question should be open-ended—that is, it should allow for more than one way of approaching or answering the question. Then, the teacher asks students to *think* about the question and spend a couple of minutes writing their thoughts about it. The students work silently and alone at this point as the teacher moves around the class examining student responses. Next, the teacher asks students to *pair* up for a couple of minutes to discuss their ideas about the question. (It's possible at this point to do a "Think-Pair-Share-Square," asking each pair to join with another pair so that each student hears from and discusses with three other students.) Finally, the teacher calls the class back together, re-poses the question, and conducts a discussion with the class as a whole so that students can *share* ideas broadly.

This strategy allows students to work with peers and addresses their need to "shift gears" during the class period to work with several shorter activities rather than sustaining attention for extended periods. It encourages students to think and formulate and defend ideas in a setting that feels safe. Because students first test out their ideas with just one other peer, it is easier for reticent students to talk. Because each student gets input from at least one other student prior to the whole-class discussion, each student is prepared to contribute to the discussion with some confidence.

Highly able middle schoolers need opportunites to talk with highly able peers to test and extend their own thinking. Therefore, it can be helpful to allow students to choose partners so that very bright students who wish to do so can pair with students who also think at an advanced level. At some points, teachers might want to assign pairs that will remain intact for a number of think-pair-shares to match such students. Assigned pairs might also be useful in ensuring that high potential students who do not perform at a high level engage with students who do perform at a high level so that the high potential students see themselves as "belonging with" achievers.

Strategy Three—New American Lecture

This strategy guides teachers in developing modified lectures that work more effectively with young adolescents than do long stretches of teacher talk while students "take notes." In the New American Lecture the teacher carefully maps out, in advance of class, the information to be shared with students, making certain that it is well organized to introduce essential knowledge, understandings, and skills. The teacher then develops a graphic organizer that follows the sequence of the lecture. The organizer guides the thinking of students who need support in following the flow of ideas as they take notes. As the class begins, the teacher opens with a "hook" question to capture the interest of students, connect with their lives, or arouse their curiosity. It begins to focus their attention on the *meaning* of what will follow. The teacher stops every six or seven minutes (the typical length of the young adolescent attention span) throughout the lecture to ask students to summarize key points, present alternative views, project what might come next, or ask questions.

This strategy is well suited to the short attention spans of many young adolescents. In addition, it helps them develop important skills of listening, synthesizing key ideas, questioning, and so on, but does so in ways that coach the students in these areas rather than assuming the students already have the skills or will develop them automatically. Used appropriately, the strategy helps students gain meaning from important content presented daily.

Some very bright middle schoolers need help in developing the skills of listening and note taking. This may be particularly true of students with high potential but lower performance. In those instances, they too will benefit from use of the graphic organizer that is typically a part of the New American Lecture. However, the organizer is a kind of scaffolding that might be likened to training wheels to help students develop advanced skills. There will be bright middle schoolers who no longer need the training wheels. They already do a competent job of listening, inferring organization, and abstracting meaning from lectures. In the case of those students, an organizer that is of great benefit to other students is actually a step backwards. A good alternative for these students might be to show them how to take two-column notes in which they record key ideas and information on the left and write their own reflections and questions on the right. Another option might be to modify the organizer so that it asks these students to make unusual connections, search for underlying concepts, uncover additional meanings or emerging patterns, or examine the material from unusual perspectives instead of focusing largely or solely on information.

Strategy Four—Teacher-Led Small-Group Instruction

In almost every middle school class, there is a considerable span of readiness levels and interests represented. To ensure maximum success for all students in that range, it is extremely helpful if a teacher develops instructional routines that include regular times to meet with small groups of varied sizes, makeups, and purposes. Based on information from student interest inventories, ongoing assessment of student progress, and student requests, the teacher plans time to meet with small groups of students to re-teach ideas and skills for students who need additional guidance, to teach ideas and skills in new ways for students not finding success with earlier ways of teaching, to connect topics of study with student interests, and to extend student thinking about important ideas and skills. Essential to the success of small-group instruction is teaching students the routines and expectations necessary for them to work appropriately on assigned tasks while the teacher is working with the small groups. Small-group instruction may take as little as five minutes or as long as 30 minutes, depending on student needs. Composition of the small groups should vary regularly based on student need and teacher intent.

> *Essential to the success of small-group instruction is teaching students the routines necessary for them to work appropriately on tasks while the teacher works with small groups.*

Mrs. Hartley enjoyed her very heterogeneous mix of seventh-grade language arts students. She found that—depending on the skill or concept being studied—students "slid" all over the spectrum of expertise; thus, ongoing assessment and small-group instruction became essential routines in her classroom. Students' responses to the exit card below (Figure 18) revealed varying degrees of readiness for using metaphors in poetry.

FIGURE 18
Sample Exit Card

Name: _____

1. What is a metaphor?
2. Give at least two examples.
3. Explain why songwriters and poets use metaphors.

Some students were honest and simply wrote "I don't know" across the card. Others could give a definition and a few shallow examples, but were unable to articulate a reason why poets and songwriters would bother with such things. Still others described some of their favorite song lyrics in depth, explaining the shades of meaning the metaphors communicated that "ordinary" language could not. Mrs. Hartley decided to form two small instructional groups in her class the following period, and when students entered the room that day, two assignments were distributed:

1. For those students with a sophisticated understanding of the use of metaphors, Mrs. Hartley assigned a "Me Metaphor" poem that pushed students to use an extended metaphor to describe themselves: *Choose something to which you'd like to compare yourself. It can be something in nature, a machine of sorts, a song, a force, an animal, a color, an emotion—the only thing it cannot be is another person. Strive for at least four stanzas (line lengths in stanzas can vary). After you've worked up some ideas, I will be around to confer with you and show you a few examples of poets who use extended metaphors in their own writing.*

2. For students who struggled to give examples of metaphors, or to articulate the reasons why poets would use them, Mrs. Hartley began with a small-group mini-lesson on metaphors and similes, giving examples to describe herself, referring to both concrete and abstract examples from poems students had already read. When students felt they were ready to work on their own, she assigned the following task: *Write a "Me Metaphor" poem in which you describe yourself using a series of metaphors and similes. You may describe both what you are and what you are not. Try using couplets, and strive for about five to seven couplets. See pages 314 and 315 in your text for more information about couplets.*

Once these students were working independently, Mrs. Hartley moved back to the advanced students—many of whom had begun their extended analogies but struggled for ways in which to continue them. Through examination of poems such as Shakespeare's "Sonnet #34" ("Why did thou promise such a beauteous day...?") and discussions of the different kinds of power wielded by abstract comparisons versus concrete comparisons, she was able to push their thinking and the sophistication of their composition in ways she would not have been able to if only addressing them in a large-group forum. At the end of the lesson, individual students had composed "Me Metaphor" poems of which they were proud and which demonstrated academic and intellectual growth; yet, each student had done so by lifting the "intellectual weights" most suitable for building his or her particular academic muscles.

Variance in student readiness, interest, and mode of learning is a given at any age. A hallmark of early adolescence is developmental variability. In any one room are students who read as well as the teacher and students who have not at all mastered the skills of independent reading, students who are abstract thinkers and students who are very concrete in their thinking, students who pay attention well and students who have great difficulty attending, students with broad and rich background experiences and students who lack context for important content they need to master, students for whom learning is easy and students who struggle with learning, students with developing interests and students with well developed interests. Variety is virtually a synonym for early adolescence. It is nearly impossible to address the needs of the full array of middle school learners with one-size-fits-all presentation, practice, or production. Small-group teaching is one of the most potent ways to address learner variance.

> ### *Small-group teaching is one of the most potent ways to address learner variance.*

Further, middle school learners need a strong sense of affiliation with their teachers. They need to feel that their teachers know them and care about their success. Small-group instruction also allows teachers to converse with, observe, and connect with individual students in a way that is difficult if whole-class instruction is the sole mode of teacher-student interaction.

Teachers who meet regularly with small groups of students have a ready-made vehicle for providing challenge for highly able middle schoolers. Small-group instruction allows teachers to engage in questioning and discussion at advanced levels with advanced students. Small groups allow teachers to use advanced materials with students who are ready for them. In small groups, teachers can present tasks, products, and rubrics designed for particular groups. Further, small groups based on shared student interests allow a teacher to extend the interests of students with well developed passions. For students with high potential and lower performance, small groups can serve a dual purpose. It's important for these students to work in teacher-led small groups that are discussing complex issues and solving complex problems. It may also be necessary for some of the same students to work in small groups that are reinforcing or re-teaching critical background knowledge or skills. In other words, small-group instruction allows a teacher to work both forward and backward with students who have high potential but may also have gaps in their learning.

Finally, just like all other middle schoolers, high-performing young adolescents need to know their teachers accept them as they are, care about them, and want to participate in their continuing growth. Teacher-led small-group instruction allows communication of these messages to very bright middle schoolers and to their peers. For students with potential to perform at high levels who do not yet exercise that potential, small-group instruction is especially potent. It allows teachers to bond with the students, keep a watchful eye on students' development, send a persistent message of high expectations and high support, and discover means of connecting students with learning.

Strategy Five—Compacting

The strategy called compacting was developed by Joe Renzulli at the University of Connecticut. It provides teachers with a structured approach to assess student knowledge and skills and plan for productive student work once a student has mastered target knowledge and skills. There are three steps in compacting. First, a teacher gives students a pre-assessment to determine the degree to which those students already have command of knowledge and skill central to an upcoming unit of study. If the teacher is relatively certain that the content is going to be new to virtually all learners, the assessment may be given a few days into the unit after highly able students have a chance to work with the information. In step two, the teacher checks the assessment, noting which goals a student has mastered and which goals the student will still need to pursue. Also in step two, the teacher notes ways in which a student might work further with those goals (for example, completing related homework assignments, taking part in a classroom demonstration on a goal). In step three, the teacher and often the student plan meaningful and productive work for the student to do while others in the class continue to work with the knowledge and skills the student who is more advanced in this area has already mastered. In the third stage, the teacher describes the nature of the student work including goals, expectations, time lines, and working requirements. In that way, a student "compacts out of" work that is redundant for that student and moves ahead to more challenging work. At the same time, if the student has some areas of weakness in the unit, step two in the process ensures that the student will work in those areas and not end up with learning gaps.

Typically, students compact out of content that is knowledge based and skills based, not work that is understanding based. In understanding-based content, all students can work with the same understandings, just at different levels of sophistication. The essential understandings in a discipline are very enduring; there's a first grade version of them and a Ph.D. version. Teachers can adjust the sophistication of understanding-based work using the Equalizer explained in Chapter 4.

There will often be students in a class who know a significant amount of material other students will need to learn but still need support in learning. Not all of these students will be identified as gifted. Often, students who are just highly motivated and work really hard like the opportunity to "test out" of material. They'll read and study in advance of the assessment so that they can have the opportunity to work with a task or product they find interesting. Any student who wants to have the chance to compact out of work should have the chance to do so.

Students can work on assignments individually as a result of compacting, but middle schoolers often enjoy "group compacting," in which pairs or small groups of students work together on tasks designed to challenge them when they compact out of content. This not only meets the need of many middle schoolers to work with peers, but can also streamline the teacher's role in designing alternate tasks.

Compacting can be a godsend for middle schoolers who are advanced in a content area. It allows them opportunities to work with tasks that are personally meaningful and challenging and still reassures the teacher that the student is proficient with required competencies. Compacting provides an arena in which teachers can help highly able students learn to work successfully at increasing levels of independence.

> *Compacting provides an arena in which teachers can help highly able students learn to work successfully at increasing levels of independence.*

In some instances, it makes sense for the work a student does in the time bought with prior mastery to be related to the topic the class is studying. So, for example, Jessica compacted out of introductory work in her sixth-grade math class on converting data into various types of graphs. She enjoyed math and as an alternative task, she researched and graphed the cost of several important purchases such as cars and homes during the lifetimes of her grandparents and parents. On the other hand, an alternative task can provide a wonderful opportunity for a student to pursue a topic of interest but which is not on the school agenda. For example, Matt was a seventh grader who was keenly interested in and very knowledgeable about anthropology. He and his teacher designed a series of connected studies based on anthropology that he pursued throughout the year when he compacted out of required content in his English class.

It is important for teachers to recall that, just like other middle schoolers, Matt and Jessica need and want their teachers' attention, interest, and support. Therefore, teachers need to make time to talk with students about the work they are doing when they are compacting out of a segment of study and provide meaningful feedback to the students on that work.

Remember, too, that these bright individuals are still young adolescents and that deep content knowledge is not always accompanied by strong organizational skills. Teachers working with students like Jessica and Matt may still need to work on procedural matters, check-in dates, research steps, and similar issues.

Strategy Six—Problem-Based Learning

Problem-Based Learning (PBL) was initially developed by Harold Barrows as a method of instructing his medical students. He was concerned that the students did not truly *understand* the curriculum. In other words, while they could recall and repeat information, he feared they were not able to transfer it to a variety of situations or to adapt it for the requirements of varied situations. These same concerns will seem familiar to many, if not all, middle school teachers. PBL is an inquiry-based approach to teaching and learning that requires students to make meaning of what they are learning, think flexibly, and apply content to address ambiguous problems.

A problem-based learning activity begins with the teacher serving as a project *guide* or "metacognitive *coach*" rather than as a *director*, dividing students into collaborative teams of five to eight students. The students are presented with a "fuzzy" problem that serves as a gateway into the investigation of essential discipline-based curricular objectives. Such problems are purposely ill-defined, because as part of the PBL learning process, students must refine the questions targeted for research. An example of a PBL question in middle school health follows.

> *A major soft drink manufacturer has volunteered to provide state-of-the-art soda machines to every middle school in our district and to split equally with the schools all profits from the sales of sodas. Should the school board accept the offer?*

Before students can generate the more precise questions or determine the roles and perspectives they will need to investigate, they consult one another and pool information in an effort to record what they know about the research topic. This step encourages students to activate prior knowledge and fosters a feeling of investment, as their personal experiences and understanding form the basis of further research.

Once students have articulated what they already know, they move to a discussion of what they need to know to solve the problem. Students document these questions in process journals or logs—tools that allow students to capture and record the development of their problem-solving process.

With these guiding questions in place, the group subdivides itself to efficiently seek out answers to its questions. Students select the question(s) or roles in which they are most interested and devise "action plans" that articulate the procedure and resources they will pursue to find information to fill in their respective pieces of the puzzle. After students have thoroughly researched their individual areas—consulting a variety of print, electronic, and human resources in the process—they come together to share their individual perspectives and synthesize their findings. If further research is needed to settle disputes or to fill in research holes, students combine efforts to locate the missing information. Ultimately, students develop a final product to both communicate their proposed solution and defend its viability with support from their research.

Middle grades students are consumed with questions such as "Who am I?" and "Where do I fit?" Because PBL is designed to meaningfully connect content to the real world, it holds great promise for stirring and holding their curiosity. The investigative process begins with students discussing what they already know, or think they know, about the topic at hand; furthermore, learners are given the chance to identify the portion(s) of the problem most intriguing to them and to search these out in more detail. Such a "divide and conquer" strategy allows students to pursue areas of interest and curiosity, increasing motivation and active investment in the research process. This opportunity to "construct knowledge" is especially important, because early adolescence is a time when students want to make sense of things for themselves. The fact that students are able to both wrestle with issues on their own and then synthesize and revise their conclusions in the context of structured peer interaction makes PBL a perfect fit for adolescents experiencing the developmental shift from focus on self to focus on the group.

Problem-based learning holds great promise for stretching bright learners because it positions them to work with complex and ambiguous ideas, advanced materials, rigorous thought, and skills of independence. Consequently, PBL tasks also call on students to deal with the ethics of decision making.

> *Problem-based learning affords teachers great flexibility in adjusting grouping, assessment, resources, and pacing to provide advanced challenge.*

PBL affords teachers great flexibility in adjusting grouping, assessment, resources, and pacing to provide advanced challenge. If advanced students are grouped homogeneously according to readiness, they may receive a problem statement with less information, guidance, or structure. In mixed-ability PBL groups, teachers can provide advanced resources to more advanced students in a very natural manner, because a variety of resources must be investigated for a team to arrive at an informed decision. Likewise, very bright students working in both homogeneous and heterogeneous teams can work with graduated rubrics and advanced, expert-like assessments. Finally, pacing can be adjusted; if a student discovers an area of interest embedded into the PBL task itself, the student has the freedom to slow down and explore that aspect in more detail while teammates pursue other avenues of the problem. Most importantly, both the problem statements and the inquiry process itself can be tweaked to allow for further adjustments to meet the needs of bright adolescents.

Strategy Seven—Complex Instruction

Complex Instruction (CI), developed by Elizabeth Cohen, is a collaborative instructional strategy that asks students to work in heterogeneous groups to complete high level tasks, drawing upon the particular strengths of each student in the group. Complex instruction tasks should be challenging, intrinsically interesting and rewarding to students, use a variety of media, and require reading and writing. Perhaps most importantly, complex instruction tasks should require a variety of talents and skills to ensure that each student makes a significant and meaningful contribution to the success of the group. Conversely, appropriate tasks will *not* have one right answer or one way to solve a problem, focus on rote learning, or be more efficiently done by one or two members of the group than by the group as a whole. Further, when students in the group speak languages other than English, materials must be in a variety of languages. Also, there must be students in a group who can speak both English and the other languages to serve as "bridges" in communication.

The teacher plays several key roles in complex instruction. As a precursor to developing complex instruction tasks, the teacher studies students to determine the particular intellectual strengths each student brings to school. The teacher then develops tasks that call upon those skills. While students work, the teacher moves among the groups engaging them in "assignment of status." This entails looking for genuine student strengths and pointing them out to the group with explanations of why the skills are important in the real world. Over time, the teacher increasingly delegates authority for planning and decision making to the group, ensuring that students learn the skills necessary to manage the authority well.

As has been the case with several other strategies, complex instruction is ideally suited to early adolescence when student curiosity is high, the desire to connect with peers is at a peak, the need to prepare for increasing independence is strong, the capacity to think in complex ways is developing, and students hunger to make sense of their world without constant adult intervention. This strategy is also effective in achieving success for all students in heterogeneous groups.

It is too often the case that in heterogeneous groups, some students always play the role of teacher and others fill the role of "the taught." Likewise, group work often focuses on drill and practice, which almost ensures that the work will be too difficult for some students and too easy for others. Cohen has dealt with this issue by requiring that tasks call on the strengths that every student brings to the table. The teacher often reminds the students, "This work cannot be completed successfully if any person in the group is missing, because that student's talents are critical to the success of the group." Further, complex instruction compliments every student in the class with the expectation that each student should be working with interesting and complex tasks. This is facilitated with the integration of multiple media and modes of expression and materials at different readability levels and, when needed, in different languages. Nonetheless, all students are called upon to read and write in the context of high interest work because those are gatekeeper skills that must be developed in each learner.

As is the case with problem-based learning, complex instruction offers teachers great flexibility in group assignments, use of varied materials, and guidance offered to students. The high level nature of complex instruction tasks is well suited to both the cognitive profiles and varied interests and learning preferences of highly able middle school students. The strategy attends to their need to be part of a group that is excited about learning. Developed appropriately, complex instruction tasks should give highly able students an opportunity to excel in their particular talent areas while developing appreciation for the talents of others.

> *Complex instruction offers teachers great flexibility in group assignments, use of varied materials, and guidance offered to students.*

Complex instruction (CI) also has great promise for students who have high ability but do not yet exhibit high performance. CI tasks are highly motivating, foster development of high level skills, promote independence, and help students see themselves and one another as intellectual contributors. Research on complex instruction shows strong achievement gains for students from low-income and culturally diverse groups after one year in complex instruction classrooms.

An Additional Suggestion or Two

The instructional strategies described in this chapter are just a few of many that, used appropriately, invigorate learning for middle school students—including highly able middle schoolers. Among other very promising and related strategies are independent study, WebQuests, and web inquiry projects (addresses provided at the end of this chapter). They are particularly useful in helping some middle school students extend their advanced abilities as thinkers, inquirers, and researchers. Many teachers use WebQuests to help students use the Internet to engage with important ideas. As is the case with many middle schoolers, some highly able middle level learners also benefit from the balance of freedom and structure provided by WebQuests. For middle school students who are more proficient with the skills of independence, a related strategy called Web Inquiry may be more beneficial. Web inquiry is also an Internet-based research process but calls on more sophisticated skills of independence and is likely to be appropriately challenging for those middle school students who are already relatively independent inquirers. Information about web inquiry projects can be found at the Web site of San Diego State University, where Bernie Dodge, Philip Molebash, and associates developed and continue to support use of WebQuests as a teaching/ learning tool. The following preview should assist teachers attempting to discern one from the other.

The WebQuest site offers myriad examples of reviewed inquiry projects designed for virtually every subject and grade level. A great asset of the WebQuest is that the process of the task is clearly outlined, the criteria for success explicitly displayed, and the Internet research sites carefully screened. Another benefit for middle grades teachers wishing to use WebQuests with bright learners is that there are differing levels of projects. Students in the same class can simultaneously work on several different quests, all revolving around the same project but stretching students of differing readiness levels. The "matrix" of examples—accessible from the site's opening page—offers a ready reference list of projects designed for both middle and secondary students. Often, the latter category offers projects of more appropriate degrees of challenge for bright middle school students than does the former.

Web Inquiry Projects (WIPs), diagrammed below (Figure 19), are a bit more open-ended than are WebQuests, and they call for students to engage in a more authentic inquiry process.

Source: http://edweb.sdsu.edu/wip/

FIGURE 19

Teachers can design their own Web Inquiry Projects or select from samples offered at San Diego State's ever-expanding resource base. Furthermore, a teacher can assign the same Web Inquiry Project to an entire class but adjust the level of challenge by providing varying levels of support or "scaffolding." The various levels of inquiry are displayed in Figure 20. Note that at the highest degree of challenge, students must develop a problem situation themselves as well as the procedure for solving the problem and the actual solution.

FIGURE 20
Levels of Web Inquiry Projects

Level of Inquiry	Problem?	Procedure?	Solution?
0	•	•	•
1	•	•	–
2	•	–	–
3	–	–	–

Source: http://edweb.sdsu.edu/wip/

Independent investigations

Mastering the skills of independence is a key developmental need for young adolescents. Some highly able middle school students are quite advanced in their ability to pose worthwhile questions for investigation, develop plans to pursue answers, use time wisely, and create authentic products of high quality. Other bright middle schoolers, much like the majority of their agemates, need structure and guidance as they grapple with and become more proficient with those skills. For students in the former group, it can be especially liberating when teachers allow them to develop plans for investigations and, with modest oversight, carry them out.

Geoff was a middle school student with very advanced knowledge of science and computers. With the encouragement of one of his teachers, he spent a year investigating theories of extinction of dinosaurs and creating computer programs to track the trajectories of meteors that might have contributed to their demise. That was a life-changing year for him and cost his teacher little in the way of time and effort. Another student, Scott, was a seventh grader whose grades skirted disaster most of the time, until a teacher encouraged his interest in comics by supporting him in writing, publishing, and marketing comic books. The teacher integrated many required language arts goals into his independent work. Scott's grades improved radically. Much later he said, "There were only two times in all of my school experience when I thought there was any place for me in the world of learning. My seventh-grade English class was one of those; and without it, I would have been lost to school, perhaps permanently." ❖

Learn More About These and Other Instructional Strategies That Are Effective in Teaching Bright Middle Grades Learners

Central Michigan University (n.d.). Effective Lecturing (Online). Retrieved September 25, 2005, from http://www.facit.cmich.edu/instructional-development/links/effectivelecturing.htm

Cohen, E. (1994). Restructuring the classroom: Conditions for productive small groups. *Review of Educational Research, 64*(1),*1–35.*

Cohen, E., Lotan, R., Whitcomb, J., Balderrama, M., Cossey, R., & Swanson, P. (1994). Complex instruction: Higher order thinking in heterogeneous classrooms. In S. Sharan (Ed.), *Handbook of cooperative learning* (pp. 82-96). Westport, CT: Greenwood Press.

Cohen, E., Lotan, R., Scarloss, B., & Arellano, A. (1999). Complex instruction: Equity in cooperative learning classrooms. *Theory into Practice, 38*(2), 80–86.

Delisle, R. (1997). *How to use problem-based learning in the classroom.* Alexandria, VA: Association for Supervision and Curriculum Development.

Gallagher, S. (2001). Adapting problem-based learning for gifted students. In F. Karnes & S. M. Bean (Eds.), *Methods and materials for teaching the gifted and talented* (pp. 369–397). Waco, TX: Prufrock Press.

Gordon, P., Rogers, A., Comfort, M., Gavula, N., & McGee, B. (2001). A taste of problem-based learning increases achievement of urban minority middle-school students. *Educational Horizons, 79,* 171-175.

Illinois Mathematics and Science Academy (2005). Problem-based-learning network: IMSA (Online). Retrieved October 31, 2005, from http://www2.imsa.edu/programs/pbln/

Reis, S., & Renzulli, J. (2003). *Curriculum Compacting: A systematic procedure for modifying the curriculum for above average ability students.* Retrieved May 30, 2006, from http://www.sp.uconn.edu/-nrcgt/sem/semart08.html

Taba, H., & Elkins, D. (1966). *Teaching strategies for the culturally disadvantaged.* Chicago: Rand McNally.

Tomlinson, C. (2003). *Fulfilling the promise of the differentiated classroom: Strategies and tools for responsive teaching.* Alexandria, VA: Association for Supervision and Curriculum Development.

Tomlinson, C., & Kiernan, L. (2003). *Instructional strategies for the differentiated classroom: Facilitator's guide.* Alexandria, VA: Association for Supervision and Curriculum Development.

Tomlinson, C., & McTighe, J. (2006). *Integrating differentiated instruction and understanding by design: Connecting kids and content.* Alexandria, VA: Association for Supervision and Curriculum Development.

Web Inquiry Homepage: http://edweb.sdsu.edu/wip/

WebQuest Homepage: http://webquest.sdsu.edu/

6

Strategies and Principles at Work in Middle School Classrooms

I love what you've done for us. You really pushed us beyond what we thought was our limit. I didn't think that I could do it, but ... I did!

—Kira, 8th Grade

Monday morning finds Mr. Ortega at his desk, simultaneously tired and rejuvenated. He has just returned from a weekend science conference where one session featured a presentation of how Problem-Based Learning could be used in the science classroom. During the session, Mr. Ortega's thoughts had immediately turned to Elijah: "This would really pique his interest!" mused Mr. Ortega. "I think this strategy might give me a way to harness Elijah's interests and strengths while drawing in his buddies who are 'on the fringe,' so to speak, because this is not a 'school-ish' activity." Mr. Ortega continued to ponder, "If I design this task correctly, this project could hit my students right where they live—relate to their real lives! They'd be able to work in groups—which they love—yet be responsible for independent investigations. It might really hook those students who feel they are 'too cool' for my regular science fare."

His contemplations cut short by the first period bell, Mr. Ortega scratches some quick notes to himself and prepares to greet his class. "I'm going to try to start this project Wednesday," he decides, "which gives me a couple of days to finalize my plans and to do some 'kid-watching;'

I want these groups to be perfect—to encourage collaboration rather than confrontation."

Wednesday morning arrives with an aura of excitement. Mr. Ortega feels he's arranged his PBL groups strategically; Elijah is in a group with one of his buddies, Lavon, a "fringe" student who is usually completely tuned out and seems to purposefully sabotage his performance and grades. Also in the group are two female students: Beth, an average student with extraordinary peacemaking abilities (she's one of eight children); and Rachel, a high achiever who struggles to "go deep" in her thinking. The other groups were formed with the same amount of deliberation and strategy, but Mr. Ortega is especially anxious to see how Elijah and Lavon do in this alternative instructional model.

"We are ready to start our new energy unit," Mr. Ortega announces. This information is met primarily with silence, interrupted only by the occasional deep sigh. "I can see that your 'cups runneth over' with excitement," jokes Mr. Ortega dryly. "What if I told you that you'll be working in groups?" This query draws whoops and high-fives from most of the eighth graders—not an unusual reaction from this highly social group. "I thought that might wake you up!" smiles Mr. Ortega. "Now, you and your teammates will be working together in a truly interdependent fashion; success on this project means that everyone—and I do mean everyone—will have to pull his or her own weight. We'll be dealing with a real issue—one that applies to you and this school and may hold connections to your own neighborhoods and families. I'm going to be asking you to step outside of the box on this assignment, and frankly, I'm excited to see what you all will accomplish!"

Mr. Ortega goes on to reveal the problem that his students will spend the greater part of the quarter investigating. He adapted it from a problem he saw at the conference, and tweaked it to better apply and appeal to this particular group of students.

> Our school is considering cutting athletic programs in order to save money. We are short on funds this year because of the high cost of heating our building; of particular difficulty is the gymnasium. If the school can save money on its heating

costs, we may not have to cut school programs. The board
is considering changing to oil heat, but some people object,
saying that it will not be as efficient or economical. You have
been asked to report to the school board on how best to
conserve energy as well as which energy source—coal, gas, oil,
or electricity—would be most economical.

(Delisle, 1997)

"Now, this is pretty open-ended. What are some of the questions rattling
around in your brains? What are you going to need to know before you
can tackle this project? Take a few minutes to mull this over, and jot down
your thoughts and questions as they pop into your heads." Silence reigns
as some students write, and others simply stare at the board. This is brand
new territory, and many are unsure how to react. Mr. Ortega takes this in
stride; he was warned about this at the conference, and he knows he will
have to take specific steps to help students—so used to memorizing and
regurgitating—to think creatively and deeply.

"Okay, before I place you in your groups, I'd like to start with a
brainstorming activity." He writes the word "energy" on the board and
circles it. "What about this concept is of concern in this situation?"
Students begin to contribute answers such as "types, resources, costs,
benefits, pollution, structures," and Mr. Ortega uses these answers to
form a concept map on the board. Some responses draw on learning from
previous units; others introduce new ideas. Mr. Ortega is pleased, because
the new ideas align with the curricular objectives he has in place for his
students, but he offers little feedback in this phase; his job is merely to
record and organize.

When students feel they have a thorough concept map, Mr. Ortega
announces, "I am going to place you in your groups. You'll each get a
packet that will serve as your problem-based learning—PBL for short—
journal. On the first page of your PBL journal, please recreate our concept
map. On the next page you'll find a Know, Need-to-Know (KNK) chart.
Work with your group members to fill in these two columns. I'll be
around to help." Mr. Ortega got the idea of the KNK chart from the Illinois
Mathematics and Science Academy (2005) Web site; as he circulates

through the groups, he attempts to scaffold students' thinking using some of the coaching techniques he found at the same site:

- Recognize and affirm students' prior knowledge.
- Recognize assumptions (expose students' thinking).
- Encourage higher order thinking.
- Encourage student participation and leadership in problem solving.
- Assist students in taking ownership of the problem.
- Make sure students don't jump to a premature conclusion.
- Keep the problem open-ended; consider many ideas and questions.
- Validate what the students know from the KNK chart.
- Refine concept map or develop new concept map, if necessary.

While talking with Elijah's group, Mr. Ortega sizes up the interaction. Rachel is definitely keeping the group on track, but, surprisingly, Lavon and Beth are doing the majority of the talking; Lavon is irritated with the school system for considering cutting the athletic program and wants to suggest alternative funding cuts rather than energy solutions. Beth counters these arguments with the idea that energy costs will continue to increase if something isn't done, and all programs will be in danger. Elijah sits, brow furrowed, taking it all in. "What are you thinking, Elijah?" asks Mr. Ortega.

"Well, I'm looking at this concept map, and I think Beth is right—it's a bigger problem than just an athletic program—but, I also think it's bigger than just a school problem."

"Explain," probes Mr. Ortega.

"Well, depending on which option we choose, we might affect the environment and the economy—there are a lot of people who still work in the mines just over the border in Pennsylvania."

Mr. Ortega remains calm on the surface, but his pulse races with excitement. This was exactly how he had planned to "up the ante" for Elijah—by leading him to discuss "...conflicting ethical appeals" (Gallagher, 2001, p. 378). "Sounds like you have some more information to add to your concept map, and to your KNK chart. Your group has a lot to crunch on!"

As Mr. Ortega moves away, he sees Lavon lean in; he knows Lavon has been considering the possibility of going to work in one of the nearby mines to earn some money for his struggling family. "It's working!" rejoices Mr. Ortega silently, as he moves on to another group.

The following week, Mr. Gerard, the GT science teacher, approaches Mr. Ortega in the cafeteria: "I saw your students in the library last week. They were really focused! And I also saw you had a group of adults in your room on Friday. What's going on?"

Mr. Ortega explains his PBL project, adding, "The panel was the kids' idea; they contacted people from the mines, the power plant, the Environmental Council, and a building contractor and asked them to come in and answer their questions!"

"They did this themselves?" exclaims Mr. Gerard.

"Well, they did use my e-mail account so that I could monitor their interactions, and we did have to discuss the proper etiquette for making contacts and requests, but they did all the legwork themselves. They are learning more about science, English, history, and math from this project than I ever imagined was possible!"

"I'd love to talk with you about how you're doing this. I have some students who are high achievers but seem to be stifled in their ability to think deeply," explains Mr. Gerard, thinking of Charlie, in particular. "It sounds like this activity would help me to curb the idea that there's one 'right' answer to everything. I see this tendency growing worse every year among my GT students."

"It certainly does address that issue," answers Mr. Ortega. "There are all sorts of ways to modify the process for your learners with high potential. Elijah, an especially insightful student who usually chooses to hide his deep thinking, found and shared connections to both the environment and the economy. I was thrilled! I think he chose to engage—and to do so at his maximum capacity—because this problem features something real, something that actually applies to him and to his typically reticent buddies, who got involved, too! I want to keep challenging Elijah, though. If I see him starting to spin his wheels, I may try to get him thinking about other extensions that, as a class, we probably won't get to—issues such as foreign trade and our dependence on other countries."

"I'm really trying to raise the ceiling in my classroom by drawing on some interdisciplinary connections," reflects Mr. Gerard (Gallagher, 2001, p. 378). This sounds ideal. Do you mind if I stop by during my planning period to see your kids at work?"

"That would be great!" responds Mr. Ortega. "Maybe we can talk after school, too; I have some great resources to share."

Complex instruction at work

Mrs. Locke, an exploratory business teacher, is tired of covering her state's competencies in a linear fashion. She feels like learning is segmented enough, due to the nature of her A-B alternating schedule, and is further fragmented by dividing up content that should be woven together into a tapestry. "I'd like to see the kids exploring more, too. After all," she silently quips, "this is an 'exploratory' course!" She surveys three of the state competencies that she usually covers individually (Figure 21), noting their natural points of intersection and overlap. "Couldn't they 'demonstrate skills that promote success in the workplace' (A2.00) while 'exploring career opportunities through job simulations' (B4.00)?" she queries. "If we investigate careers in this way, students should naturally 'analyze the relationship between self-awareness and career choices' (C6.00). That settles it! I'm doing something different!" Mrs. Locke turns to her filing cabinet and locates her materials on complex instruction from a professional development session she attended. It seemed overwhelming at the time, but now upon reflection, she thinks she will be able to make it work.

The following Monday, Mrs. Locke presents her surprised and rather leery students with group placements. She spent some time over the weekend looking at her students' grades in her class and in their core classes and thinking about how they had performed in other tasks she had given them. She had been surprised to see Domenic's grade in math. "He does so well on my math-based warm-ups!" she thinks, "He could solve those career-oriented story problems with his hands tied behind his back!" She decides to go with her observations rather than with the hard data in this case, hoping her gamble will pay off. "Domenic is such a quiet,

FIGURE 21

Complex Instruction Example: "Career Development" Competencies

A—The World of Work

2.00	Demonstrate skills that promote success in the workplace
2.01	Demonstrate personal qualities (e.g., getting along with others) that are needed to obtain and keep jobs.
2.02	Explain the importance of interpersonal relationships skills and teamwork on the job.
2.03	Apply problem-solving skills to real-life situations in the workplace.

B—Exploring Career Opportunities

4.00	Explore career opportunities through job simulations
4.04.06.07.09	Explore job tasks and career opportunities in the pathways of arts and sciences, business technologies, commercial and artistic production technologies, engineering technologies.

C—Career Planning

6.00	Analyze the relationship between self-awareness and career choices.
6.02	Interpret assessment of personal interests, aptitudes, attitudes, learning styles, work values, multiple intelligences, personality, and abilities as they relate to career choices.
6.03	Examine reasons for knowing oneself before making career decisions.

Source: North Carolina Career Development Competencies

---

respectful young man. I would really like to see him be successful—his eyes just shine when he feels good about himself."

Mrs. Locke divides the class into groups of five or six, then gives them an icebreaking exercise to complete, explaining, "Each group is going to have to work together like a well-oiled machine for this project. You can't do that unless all of the machine's parts are working together—until you know a little more about one another, such as the things you're interested in, your strengths, your weaknesses, how you're similar, and how you're different." She gives each student a paper with a T-shirt copied on both the front and back. "You'll notice," she explains, "that you each have a T-shirt outline with both a front and a back side to it. Your job is to design a 'team jersey' representing who you all are. Use the directions on the board to help you. You'll have about 15 to 20 minutes to complete the following task" (Figure 22):

Figure 22

Community Building Activity to Prepare for Complex Instruction Collaboration

Design a team jersey including a team name that you devise as well as a representation of at least two things you all have in common (not obvious or visible). Also include one item that's unique to each "player." You may use words or art and include interests, experiences, strengths, weaknesses, likes, and dislikes.

Mrs. Locke circulates while the students work. The conversations are stilted at first, but eventually students warm up to each other and engage in animated conversations punctuated with laughter and exclamations such as "Me too!" and "No way!"

"This is serving its purpose," she notes with pleasure. "Not only are they getting to know one another so that they can work together better, but they are also building the foundation for the division of labor this task will demand."

After about 20 minutes, Mrs. Locke gives each group a chance to present and explain its jersey. This time of sharing is interesting and quite revealing. She then distributes an exploratory complex instruction task card to each group (Figure 23).

FIGURE 23

"Gymboree" Task Card

As a group, you are responsible for completing the following task. You have a week in which to complete this task, so make sure you budget and divide your time wisely. Remember, because of time constraints and the various talents needed to complete this task, the participation of all group members is critical to the timely and successful completion of this task.

To complete this task, you will need to identify among you:

- Someone who likes to organize and coordinate people and events
- Someone with excellent mathematical skills
- Someone who is adept at Web research
- Someone with a knack for drafting or design layout
- Someone with an artistic flair
- Some who is a good (clear and effective) writer, preferably with strong word-processing skills.

The Group's Task

Our middle school has just received a generous donation earmarked for the construction of a new gymnasium. They want this new structure to truly reflect our school's student body, so they have selected this class to submit several designs for the new gymnasium. Each group will develop its own proposal. You will need to spend some time brainstorming together about an ideal gymnasium in terms of appearance, facilities, and size. Ultimately, you will have to tailor your design to meet your allotted budget of $_____. Once you've come up with a shared vision, it's time to "divide and conquer."

1. Create an outline of the materials you will need to complete the job.
2. Research the cost of materials, labor, and similar facilities.
3. Devise a detailed budget displaying how much money you will allot for the various materials necessary to complete the job.
4. Sketch a layout of the proposed facility. This blueprint should be drawn to scale and should include labels of all the important aspects of the gymnasium.
5. Create prototypes (to scale) of two mural designs—one for one of the gym walls, and one for the floor (center court and sidelines).
6. Synthesize all of this information into a well-written and professional-looking report. Your report should contain all of the components listed above as well as an explanation for your decisions (cost, importance, meaning). Include charts and graphs, as you will make a formal presentation to the decision committee—our principal, the boys' basketball coach, the girls' volleyball coach, and one school board member.

There is a buzz as students read their cards. "This is so cool!" exclaims one student. Several others chime in with agreement. Others are not so pleased, "How are we supposed to know how to do this?" complains one. "Yeah, I don't have the slightest idea how to even start!" wails another.

"You'll have to rely on one another," soothes Mrs. Locke. "It's true—not one of you in this classroom has all the talent, knowledge, or resources required to complete this task alone. Then again, each and every one of you possesses unique gifts, knowledge, and skills that are necessary to successfully complete this project. You're going to have to rely on one another, and you're going to have to use many resources, books and magazines, the Internet, and people. I will help you and guide you, but you need to ask me targeted questions that show you've done some research. 'What are we supposed to do?' is **not** a valid question! So … put your heads together, and get rolling!"

As the week progresses, Mrs. Locke notes with pleasure that the majority of her students are hard at work and very invested. They all seem motivated by being able to choose their areas of expertise, having something original to contribute to the group, and by the knowledge that they would be presenting to a real audience—including the principal! Students are making regular trips to the library, searching the Web with focus and purpose, and using experts in their building (e.g., a math teacher, the technical education teacher who is a carpenter on the side). Mrs. Locke also notes that several students have interviewed friends or family members; they pull their group members together in hushed excitement to share what they have discovered.

Of special significance to Mrs. Locke is that Domenic has excelled in his starring role as the group's mathematician and architect. The students are so impressed, they tell their math teacher, Ms. Grand, who stops by Mrs. Locke's room after school one day. Mrs. Locke explains the project and shares some student work samples, including some of Domenic's sketches and figures.

"This is amazing," Ms. Grand responds. "I need to go dust off that folder—I went to that professional development workshop, too. I think I have the beginning of an idea that would allow me to harness the creativity of my absent-minded professor, Ray, while giving Julia a chance to see some practical implications for what we're doing. I think she's floundering in our current, strictly theoretical environment."

Mrs. Locke moved the due date ahead because students were working so hard, and because they were actually covering more competencies than she had anticipated. Later, the esteemed panel of judges arrives to evaluate the projects. They are impressed with what they see and hear, and the students are proud of their work. Before ending the unit, Mrs. Locke distributes this exit card:

Figure 24

1. What have you learned about yourself in terms of the following?
   a. Interests
   b Strengths
   c. Weaknesses
   d. Learning and working style(s)
 	
2. What have you learned about teamwork in the work world? Your ability to function as a team member?
 	
3. What have you learned about possible career fields of interest?
 	
4. By what were you most surprised during this project?
 	
5. What suggestions do you have for me for the next time I use a project such as this?

She wants to give students a chance to reflect, not only on what they have learned about the content, but on what they have learned about themselves. *She* has learned a great deal about *them*, as well, and will be sad to see them leave for their next exploratory rotation.

The Parallel of Practice at work in humanities classrooms

"Here we go!" declares Ms. Roberts, as she and Mr. Wellman sit down to the initial planning phase of their mandatory interdisciplinary unit. They have paired together in the past; each teaching team is required to provide evidence that at least two teachers have team taught an interdisciplinary unit. To do this, Ms. Roberts, the English teacher, typically supplements Mr. Wellman's history curriculum by assigning a novel set in the time period his history class is studying. She just couldn't get excited about their typical approach this year; however, maybe it was because of the strikingly vivid diversity (in readiness, interests, and cultures) of her classes, or maybe she was simply excited about the innovative things she had been trying this year. Whatever the cause, Ms. Roberts felt it was time to step out and try something new. She had learned about *The Parallel Curriculum's* (2002) "Parallel of Practice" in her annual summer graduate course, and this teaching model really got her creative juices flowing. She saw the power of asking her students to act as poets, authors, playwrights, and literary critics. She thought Mr. Wellman might enjoy this change of scenery, too. He was resistant, at first; he felt his traditional approach was tried and true. He reasoned, however, that Ms. Roberts had flexed for him so often in the past, that maybe it was time he flexed for her a bit, too.

When she first mentioned this new approach, Ms. Roberts watched a cloud descend over Mr. Wellman's face; this was clearly out of his comfort zone. She had grown so accustomed to thinking this way, that she forgot the time and effort it took to arrive at her current philosophical "resting place." The two teachers went online and looked up a job description of sorts for an historian:

> The process of historical analysis is a difficult one, involving investigation and analysis of competing ideas, facts, and purported facts to create coherent narratives that explain 'what happened' and 'why or how it happened.' (Lexico, 2005)

"So how can I get my students to investigate," asked Mr. Wellman, "when the textbook has laid it all out nicely and neatly for them—and from one perspective? Furthermore," he continued, "my standards documents are pretty clear about what I'm to cover in the period spanning World War II to the present. That's a lot of material; I'm not sure I have time for anything extra."

"It won't be 'extra,'" countered Ms. Roberts, "it will be the same *material* but from a different *approach.* I've been reading a lot about how people learn, and I think we'll actually be giving our kids an edge on the standards tests because we'll be teaching them how to think like historians and authors. With that scaffolding structure in their brains, they'll have a much better chance of retaining information they discover, and dealing with new material they've not yet encountered. They'll be able to extrapolate and to make educated inferences. That's what real historians do; they don't memorize facts about a lot of different eras or cultures—they specialize in one discrete field! And yet," she continued passionately, "they all become experts in one particular domain— historical literacy. This article," she continued, picking up a dog-eared journal from her desk, "puts it this way:"

> Historical literacy is a way of thinking about text that allows us to find truth in the cacophony of voices that confront us in the social world. To ask where information comes from and why texts are written is to confront the written word as an empowered agent, not a passive consumer. It is a form of literacy no less important in deciphering a text written in 1775 than it is when reading about war policy in Iraq in the *National Review* or in *The American Prospect,* or for that matter, when listening to Bill Moyers on PBS or Bill O'Reilly on Fox News Channel. Knowing how to read and think in this way is a survival kit for democratic life. (cited in Wineburg, 2005, p. 662)

"You see, even though the historians may not know the *facts* of time periods outside of their jurisdictions, they do know the *principles* behind gathering them and making sense of them; that *transfer power* is what helps them to navigate successfully within unfamiliar content" (Bransford, Brown, & Cocking, 2000).

"Okay, okay! Calm down! I said I'd try it!" laughed Mr. Wellman. "I have to admit, though," he said, growing sober again, "I'm not sure if I fully understand what historians do or even the nature of the guiding principles behind my discipline!"

"I'll bet you do," countered Ms. Roberts, "You just haven't had a chance to reflect upon them or articulate them. If you had to boil history down to its barest bones, what would they be? What drives human behavior?"

"Conflict," answered Mr. Wellman, decidedly. "Every historical event that we study was precipitated and perpetuated by some sort of conflict."

"Okay, so we'll write 'conflict' at the top of this page. Now, when you say 'conflict,' what kind of conflict are you talking about? We study internal and external conflicts (e.g., against self, others, and nature) in English; does that apply to history?"

"Absolutely, all of the above. People have battled the elements and famine and have struggled to survive, uprooting families and whole communities in search of literal and figurative 'greener pastures.' They've also waged war because of differing fundamental beliefs as well as the quest for power. Take, for example, the original colonists; they came here because of the conflict between their value system and that of the Church of England. Consider Hitler, the Crusades, and the Conquistadors! So, I'd say it's all of the above."

"Excellent!" mused Ms. Roberts, busily adding branches to the word "conflict," webbing the ideas Mr. Wellman had just discussed. "So, if you could reduce the source of these conflicts to two things, what would they be?"

"Hmm. … That's a little more difficult. Let me see that web." He studied it for a moment. "Well," he began, "it seems as if all of these conflicts stem either from a difference in beliefs—or values, might be a better word, because that would include the idea of 'power'—or, they were directly related to a struggle to survive."

"Okay, 'values' and 'survival'," Ms. Roberts busily wrote and circled those words, redrawing lines in the process. "So, the next question is, *What were the results of these conflicts?*"

Mr. Wellman paused and again studied the web. "I believe each of them resulted in either deterioration or progress … even invention, in many cases.

"Okay," said Ms. Roberts, scratching a few more words on their concept map. "How does this look?" (See p. 119.)

"Bravo!" exclaimed Mr. Wellman. I hadn't thought of 'reorganization,' but that's certainly true—especially in government. I also like how you connected the concept of 'power' to that of 'survival.' Actually, we could draw quite a few more connections like that—such as, in man's quest to acquire power, he may deplete or destroy valuable resources."

"You're right," sighed Ms. Roberts. "We've got to stop somewhere, though; we could ask the kids to make further connections for us."

"You mean the students will see this? I thought it was just for us."

"Technically, it's for both—for us to get our planning straight and for the kids to see how knowledge is arranged within the discipline."

Mr. Wellman paused for a moment. "What if I put this on a PowerPoint slide (Figure 25) and animate the different parts? I could reveal them as students bring them up in class discussion, and I could ask them to draw additional connections—like the power-resource connection you and I discussed a minute ago."

FIGURE 25

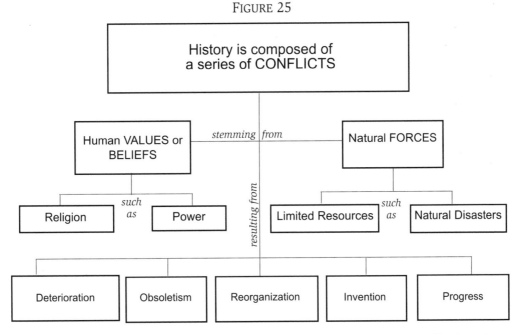

"I think that's a great idea. What would you do to get kids to talk about the map in terms of actual historical events?"

"How about if we discuss a couple of events that we've already studied but discussed them in terms of how they relate to the concept map? We could do the first one as a class; then, the students could get into small groups and repeat the process with another previously studied historical event. We could compare their multiple interpretations of the same event, and that would set us up to talk about what historians do—sift through multiple interpretations in an attempt to accurately reconstruct a past reality."

"Again, that sounds great! A good way to both review and preview! I could do the same thing with some of the stories we've read in English class; I'm thinking of *The Diary of Anne Frank*, in particular, or some of the novels from our last literature circles unit. Each of those novels featured a child narrator (for example, *Roll of Thunder, Hear my Cry* and *To Kill a Mockingbird*), and we focused on the reliability of the storyteller; we examined how the author's perspective influenced what was included and excluded from the story."

"So, is that how we're going to forge a connection between our classes—by using the concept map?"

"To begin with, anyway, but I think we can do better than that. I thought we could look at these same concepts in English, but instead of looking backward, we'd project them forward and study how these ideas apply to the genre of science fiction. We'll use the tools and methods that science fiction authors use—examining patterns of human behavior and values both in the past and the present; predicting the implications of those values and behaviors on the future; examining the value we place on technology—and we'll write futuristic stories with all the conventions of science fiction writing we encounter in our studies," explained Ms. Roberts.

"Wow! That does tie in well; it's not a forced connection at all. Could you start by discussing stories from the historical periods we discuss in our opening activity? I'm thinking we'll discuss Reconstruction as a class—that's where we began this year—and then I'll have them, either independently or in small groups, work on the United States' involvement in World War II—that's the unit we just finished."

"Let me see—the 1860s and 70s? That's pretty early for science fiction … but it was during that time period that technology started booming, so there are tons of examples of *progress* and *invention*—Edison's microphone and phonograph, the light bulb, the first transcontinental railroad, and the first and second law of thermodynamics. Jules Verne was actually quite busy, too, writing about various journeys—*A Journey to the Center of the Earth* (1864), *From the Earth to the Moon* (1865), and *20,000 Leagues Under the Sea* (1870).

"Are you sure about *20,000 Leagues* being written in 1870? They didn't even use ocean-going submarines until the 1890s."

"Yeah, that's the funny thing about science fiction; it seems to both reflect the past and, at times, predict the future! Don't look at me like that! I've been reading up on science fiction since I first started thinking about this unit!"

"You're not becoming a Trekkie, are you?"

"Well, actually, true science fiction buffs scorn *Star Trek* because of its misuse of the concept of hyperspace, as well as …"

"Okay! I've heard enough!" laughed Mr. Wellman. "Can we get back to the unit? How's it going to look, practically speaking?"

"Sorry," grinned Ms. Roberts. "So Jules Verne ties into Reconstruction in terms of both *progress* and *values*—we can see real-world technological developments as well as genuine human desire for "escape" reflected in his writings. World War II … hmmm … well, the atom bomb spawned many stories featuring the end of the world; in addition, the emergence from the war ushered in the age of the cold war, right? George Orwell wrote *1984* in 1947. That's pretty reflective of the results of one conflict bringing about the *reorganization* that produces a new and different conflict."

"Perfect! So, where do we go from there?" asked Mr. Wellman.

"I was thinking—now, shoot this down if it doesn't work—but I was thinking that you could divide your classes into teams, each serving as historians for a meaningful 'chunk' of history from the time line you're supposed to cover in this unit …"

"… and I could let the students decide which 'chunk' they're most interested in. They could work in interest-based groups to see how their period looks when organized according to the concept map. They would have to look at that time period through a variety of lenses, though, to glean a true picture of the sources and results of the major conflicts of their time period; I'll have to do some major research to find primary sources representing different perspectives for each of those time periods."

"True, but they can do some searching on their own, too. They'll have to research how their findings from history relate to science fiction written during those same time periods. That way, when we prepare to write and publish our own stories reflective of the *conflicts, values, progress,* and *deterioration* of our own day and age, we'll have a clearer picture of how to portray them."

They settled into planning a scope and sequence for their unit and deciding how to divide up historical periods, stories, and resources. Emerging from this process, they were thrilled with the results; they felt their students would react with equal enthusiasm.

"I can't believe the change in Heather!" commented Mr. Wellman in a team meeting the following week. "She's usually completely tuned out in class, but I would venture to say that she is leading the charge in her group's investigation of the Sputnik era. She is so curious and insightful; I wonder why I've never seen that before?"

"Yes, Heather struggles to pay attention during direct instruction. Sometimes I think she's just plain bored; other times, I get the feeling she's preoccupied with social concerns—you know, she's not exactly the most popular girl in her grade, as bright as she is. She's different, and middle school girls, in particular, can be ruthless when they encounter difference," reflected Ms. Roberts sadly.

"Well, she's certainly the 'Pied Piper' in her investigation group. I've got her with Brittany, who is popular, as well as Luke, Mr. Athlete, and Noah, and the four of them are operating like a well-oiled machine. I wonder," mused Mr. Wellman, "if it's because they all picked Sputnik as their first choice, so they have that in common?"

"That could very well be," answered Ms. Roberts. "I've found," she continued, "that when I approach subject matter in this way—where the kids have the responsibility of constructing knowledge themselves and must actually draw and support conclusions about the content—that they are genuinely more invested. Heather has really blossomed in these situations; I think she's naturally inquisitive, and being able to discover knowledge and draw connections really motivates her—her gifts bubble to the surface. I mean, I knew she was bright, but she's blown me away recently!"

"Talk about being blown away—Noah is a new man!" laughed Mr. Wellman. "You should see him; if the group mentions it might need a resource, he dashes off to find it, bringing it back as if it were the password to disarm a bomb!"

Ms. Roberts laughed, "Is he the 'chart master' in your class, too?"

"Oh yes, he is! He reminds me of John Madden and his chalk drawings. He stands up at the group's concept map with a thousand different-colored markers and somehow captures everything the group throws out to him."

"Yes, he's 'active,' to put it mildly. It's so fun to see what he can do when his energy is channeled! Of course, his spelling leaves a lot to be desired, but I'll bet Brittany helps him out in that arena."

"She sure does," responded Mr. Wellman. "Luke helps him stay organized, too. I've enjoyed seeing Luke spread his wings a bit. He's your typical high achiever, but I've never seen him with his brow furrowed; he's really being challenged by this!"

"Good for him! How is Jasmine doing?"

"There's another surprise," replied Mr. Wellman, shaking his head. "You know, I always marvel at her comments in response to her classmates' discussion of material they've read; it's like she hasn't read it, but can pick up on what's going on from the discussion swirling around her. Of course, her oral feedback in no way resembles anything she turns in on paper; her writing is atrocious! Most of the time I don't get a chance to see what's going on in her head. But she's a deep thinker, that one! She's in one of the civil rights groups. I had a lot of folks who were interested in that topic and formed several subgroups. Jasmine is doing interviews with her family and church members, and kind of directing her group's progress, suggesting resources, and making amazing connections. I've learned more about her in these past few weeks than I think I have all year long! I usually focus on her struggles rather than on her strengths, because I'm always worried about how she'll perform on the tests."

"I think you'll find that she'll do better on the test since she's made sense of the information in her own way—it's 'in there;' it's just a matter of getting it out! She has to do an individual assessment at the end, right?"

"Yes, each group will have two days to teach the class about its topic; class members will be responsible for completing their own concept map on how they see the time periods fitting into that schematic. I still want them to take my objective test to see how their performance measures up to my original approach to this unit. I will, however, assign an equally weighted assessment for which each student will have to either write a position paper, design a series of charts or graphs, or develop a series of illustrations tracing how our government has changed to reflect our changing values *and* projecting what our country's government may look like if we continue to cling to the values reflected in the most recent eras. I'm allowing them to use computers, as that's more authentic, and Jasmine is really excited about being able to graph her findings on the computer; her confidence level has risen dramatically during this unit. I'm still worried about the objective standardized test, though."

"Yes, that's always a hurdle. You might want to encourage her to use her answer sheet or scratch paper to cover up everything but the question she's working on. When there are fewer words swimming around on the page, she seems to be able to focus and perform better."

"I'll try that," Mr. Wellman replied. "You know, this unit has been a lot of work, but it's been worth it to see the kids really engaged and genuinely thinking for a change. Usually, I feel as if I'm in the room throwing balls out at the crowd, and they're doing nothing to try to catch them. It's as if the balls are just bouncing off their heads and rolling around the classroom floor. In this unit, it's as if that concept map and the understandings it communicates are acting as Velcro in students' brains. What's even more exciting is that they are gathering up the balls themselves and sticking them to their own brains! I know it will take a while before I can teach like this exclusively, but I'm starting to think about ways that I can incorporate little bits of this approach into my classroom routines all year long."

"Fabulous!" answered Ms. Roberts. "I'm motivated to do so, too. It has been such a joy to see kids like Ashley and Jasmine and Jonathan transcend their deficits and rise to meet their true potential." ❖

Learn More About Parallel Curriculum

Bransford, J.D., Brown, A.L., & Cocking, R.R. (Eds.). (2000). *How people learn: Brain, mind, experience, and school* (Expanded Edition). Washington, DC: National Academy Press.

Donovan, M.S., & Bransford, J.D. (Eds.). (2005). *How students learn: History, mathematics and science in the classroom*. Washington, DC: The National Academies Press.

Erickson, H. (2002). *Concept-based curriculum and instruction: Teaching beyond the facts*. Thousand Oaks, CA: Corwin Press.

Lexico Publishing Group (2005). *Wikipedia* (Online), Retrieved November 3, 2005, from http://www.reference.com/browse/wiki/Historian

Tomlinson, C.A., Kaplan, S.N., Renzulli, J.S., Purcell, J., Leppien, J., & Burns, D. (2002). *The Parallel Curriculum: A design to develop high potential and challenge high ability learners*. Thousand Oaks, CA: Corwin Press.

Tomlinson, C., & McTighe, J. (2006). *Integrating differentiated instruction and understanding by design: Connecting kids and content*. Alexandria, VA: Association for Supervision and Curriculum Development.

Wiggins, G., & McTighe, J. (1998). *Understanding by design*. Alexandria, VA: Association for Supervision and Curriculum Development.

Wineburg, S. (2005). What does NCATE have to say to future history teachers? Not much. *Phi Delta Kappan, 86,* 658–680.

Learn More About Problem-Based Learning

Delisle, R. (1997). *How to use problem-based learning in the classroom*. Alexandria, VA: Association for Supervision and Curriculum Development.

Gallagher, S. (2001). Adapting problem-based learning for gifted students. In F. Karnes, & S. M. Bean (Eds.), *Methods and materials for teaching the gifted and talented* (pp. 369-397). Waco, TX: Prufrock Press.

Gordon, P., Rogers, A., Comfort, M., Gavula, N., & McGee, B.(2001). A taste of problem-based learning increases achievement of urban minority middle-school students. *Educational Horizons, 79,* 171-175.

Illinois Mathematics and Science Academy. (2005). Problem-Based Learning Network: IMSA. (Online). Retrieved October 31, 2005, from http://www2/imsa.edu/programs/pbln/

Learn More About Complex Instruction

Cohen, E. (1994). Restructuring the classroom: Conditions for productive small groups. *Review of Educational Research, 64*(1), 1–35.

Cohen, E., Lotan, R., Whitcomb, J., Balderrama, M., Cossey, R., & Swanson, P. (1994). Complex instruction: Higher order thinking in heterogeneous classrooms. In S. Sharan (Ed.), *Handbook of cooperative learning* (pp. 82-96). Westport, CT: Greenwood Press.

Cohen, E., Lotan, R., Scarloss, B., & Arellano, A. (1999). Complex instruction: Equity in cooperative learning classrooms. *Theory into Practice, 38(2),* 80-86.

Tomlinson, C., & Kiernan, L. (2003). *Instructional strategies for the differentiated classroom: Facilitator's guide.* Alexandria, VA: Association for Supervision and Curriculum Development.

7

Some Frequently Asked Questions About Teaching Bright Kids in the Middle Grades

I guess I'm a little embarrassed to say that I have found working with really bright kids to be a bit of a cultivated taste—like for olives or artichokes or something. But in the end, I've really learned to love them and to realize that acquiring the taste has made my life richer. It's funny, but I guess they were teaching me all the time I was figuring out how to teach them, and in learning about them, I've learned a lot about myself.   —Science teacher, 7th grade

There are so many interesting facets of teaching in general and so many questions teachers ponder about teaching. We want to address a few commonly posed questions about teaching high ability and high potential students in the middle grades and hope that the brief answers we provide help extend the understanding of some of the teachers who will help shape their lives during the critical middle school years. There's a great deal more to be said about each question than there is space available, but perhaps the answers here will prompt additional thought, discussion, and study about these bright students.

1. Won't smart kids make it on their own?

When teachers ask this question, there is often a subtext stated or implied. It goes something like this: "I have so many students with 'real' problems who need me and a fixed amount of time in the day. Bright kids do well in school anyhow. I can't be everything to everybody, and if I have to skimp on attention to someone, these students seem the least likely to be harmed by that."

The truth is that some bright kids will do "fine" without us—if, by that, we mean they'll make good grades, get good test scores, and go on to college. Even these students, however, need teachers in their lives who affirm and enjoy their abilities during the formative years of early adolescence. They need teachers who show them how to develop those abilities and help them navigate the necessarily rough waters of growing up. Without those things, even the students who appear to do "fine" with little support have a middle school experience that is, in fact, impoverished.

There are also many other bright middle schoolers who don't do "fine" by any measure without focused, persistent, positive intervention from their teachers. They become alienated from an institution that doesn't seem to see them. They opt for peer approval at the cost of academic performance. They don't know how to make friends and suffer from isolation. They don't learn to study, or to persist, and the cost of not learning those things will likely be great.

The truth is—and it's actually a wonderful truth for teachers—all kids of every kind needs teachers who see them, accept them, affirm them, enjoy them, stretch them, model for them, stand beside them, and cheer them on. Any student who lacks those experiences for a significant time will be less than he or she might have been and ought to have been.

2. Isn't it unfair if I ask different kids to do different work?

We don't require all middle schoolers to wear the same size clothes, to eat the same amount of food at lunch, or to participate in the same extracurricular activity. We parent best and teach best when we try our hardest to provide what each young person needs to thrive. One teacher of adolescents explained that, in his class, students understood that doing different work or working in different ways was the norm. "In here," he said, "there's no stigma about being different. Everyone is different—that's our norm."

3. Won't bright kids (and their parents) resent it if I ask them to work harder than other kids?

Some bright kids and their parents are eager for teachers who provide challenge. Not only will these students and parents not be angry about the challenge, they'll be immensely grateful for the teachers who provide it.

There may be some parents who bristle at the notion that their child is doing work that seems harder than the work assigned to other students. It's important for teachers to listen to those parents, share the school's and the teachers' goals, and be able to reflect several beliefs to the parents in a positive way.

> *Not acknowledging a child's ability and not participating in extending it would be malpractice.*

First, when we ask bright kids to do work that's a little too hard for them, we're asking them to do exactly what we're asking every other student to do. Highly able students have a more advanced starting point than other students—but we're only asking them to stretch a little bit into discomfort. That's what we must ask every student to do if we are to be catalysts for that student's growth. Second, we need to be able to say that our goal is to ensure that the students succeed at a new level of proficiency—not fail at that new level. Therefore, we'll coach the students for success, provide clear rubrics for quality, review drafts of student work or allow appropriate opportunities for revisions. Third, we need to be able to articulate that we are talent developers, just as coaches are. Not acknowledging a child's ability and not participating in extending it would be malpractice. Fourth, it is sometimes helpful to point out to parents of bright middle schoolers that this is the perfect time to help their children learn to be excellent students—learn to study intelligently, persist in the face of difficulty, strive for high quality. That learning process can be difficult whenever it happens, especially for students who have always done well with little effort. It is safer and more humane, however, to guide bright kids through that process when parents and teachers are there to help them than it would be to wait until they are away in college, with no one to provide similar support.

Parents of bright students—and the students themselves—generally respond well to teachers who provide challenge, as long as they know the teacher values the student, is on the student's side, and is willing to listen.

4. Is it ever appropriate for bright middle school students to skip a grade?

The short answer to that question is *yes.* Research suggests that this sort of acceleration can be very productive for bright students. The longer answer is that parents, teachers, and the student in question need to look carefully at the young person as a whole. Emotional maturity, physical maturity, social readiness, and other factors will necessarily figure into making a decision about grade skipping. Some students will be best served by skipping a grade. Some will be best served by moving up a year in one subject—math for example—but staying with agemates for the rest of the day. Some will be best served by teachers who provide appropriate challenge within classes at their age and grade level. The decision to skip a grade is all about making a choice with the best "positive to negative" ratio for a given student at a given time.

5. Isn't it possible to put too much academic pressure on bright middle schoolers?

Yes, it is possible. When a student feels inordinate pressure over a sustained period, outcomes are not likely to be positive. It can lead to bouts with perfectionism, to underachievement, to rebellion against parents or school or both—a whole host of unhealthy and unpleasant options.

It is also possible to put too little academic pressure on middle schoolers and to let them coast when they could develop far more positive and productive academic behaviors and habits. There are at least three key habits of mind necessary for highly able young people to "grow into themselves." Those three are (1) persistence in the face of difficulty, (2) intellectual risk taking, and (3) creative or flexible thinking. Allowed to coast academically during the middle grades, it's unlikely that bright students will develop these key traits. What they *are* likely to develop is a sense of "entitlement"—a belief that they should get good grades because of who they are, not because of what they produce—and a belief that excellence is unrelated to effort.

As with most things, finding the right balance of pressure and autonomy is the key—and tricky. Parents and teachers need to study the bright middle schoolers whom they share, looking for signs of an imbalance. They need to work as partners to give these developing young people an academic "push" when it seems called for and to "back off" when that seems wise. Most importantly, they need to help the student learn to develop an increasing sense of autonomy as a learner and the ability to make wise choices about academics and other facets of life.

6. Some of my very able students shut down when I give them challenging work. What's going on there?

Bright middle schoolers usually found great success at the elementary school level with only modest effort. A big part of their identity has probably become associated with academic success. In middle school, academics can become much more demanding. Some of these students never learned how to study. They've seldom encountered work they can't readily do, and they don't know how to handle it when that happens. Somewhere inside them is a fear that if they can't be immediately successful with assignments, they might not be smart, after all. Close behind follows the fear that perhaps people (parents, teachers, grandparents, friends) won't like them if they aren't smart. After all, that's what people have talked about a lot in the past. On the heels of that uncomfortable thought is the question, "If I'm not smart, what am I?" Those are difficult musings at any age. They are potentially terrifying in early adolescence when nothing in life seems to be secure. It's much easier for a bright middle school student to scoff at a difficult assignment or get angry with a teacher who created it than to give voice to or try to deal with those misgivings.

Of course, that doesn't mean teachers shouldn't challenge bright middle schoolers. Rather, it means teachers need to understand what may lie beneath "refusal" of challenge and work to help the student move past the refusal. There are many factors that can help students get "unstuck" and move ahead. If work is both interesting and challenging, students may be more likely to stick with it. If they have some meaningful choices related to the work, that might help. Sometimes it makes a difference if students can work together on a task. Maybe the secret will be having the student turn in work for preliminary review with an opportunity to revise the work prior to a final submission.

Whatever it takes, many bright students learn to value challenge in a three-stage process. First, they have to encounter it regularly. Then, they have to learn to tolerate it—learn that they can prevail and that they have and can develop the resources necessary to succeed with it. Finally, they learn to embrace challenge because it gives them a sense of self-efficacy to tackle something that initially seemed beyond their reach and to prevail. Teachers in the middle grades are a critical part of all three stages.

7. I just don't have time to answer all the questions some of my bright kids ask. How can I handle that?

Some teachers are uncomfortable with questions bright kids ask because they don't know the answers to them. Somehow, as teachers, we've been groomed to believe we're supposed to have all the answers—to be the one in the front of the room who provides all the information. That being the case, it's intimidating to have young teenagers posing questions for which we have no answers. But it can be really liberating to come to the point of saying, "I don't have to know everything. I just have to recognize a good question and encourage looking for answers." It's just fine to say to a student, "Wow! I have no idea what the answer to that is—but I'd love to know. How can you find some information on that? And when you find it, will you share it with us?"

Sometimes, we struggle, as teachers, with bright kids who have boundless mental energy and "take up too much space" in classroom discussions—meaning they are so hungry to talk about ideas that they have trouble sharing the floor with other students. In those cases, it's okay to talk privately with the student about the issue. The message needs to be that you really enjoy the student's thinking and his contributions, but you also worry about the fact that sometimes other students become quiet and just wait for that student to do all the answering. Ask the student to help you figure out how to find a balance. Perhaps the student can occasionally write to you in a "thought log" and you can respond. Perhaps the student can come in before school to talk with you about ideas. The goal is to encourage the student's thinking, encourage him or her to be aware of the needs of others, and find a balance.

> *If we are pressured to "get through" the curriculum at the expense of addressing student questions and at the cost of silencing student voices, we will lose more than we gain.*

Sometimes the issue is that the teacher feels there is little time to do anything but "cover the curriculum," leaving no time for students' questions. That's a tougher issue. In a time of high stakes testing, it's easy to understand the pressure a teacher feels to make sure students "get through" the curriculum. However, if we do that at the expense of addressing student questions and at the cost of silencing student voices, we will lose more than we gain. Perhaps we could reserve a few minutes at the end of each class for student questions and discussions, or perhaps students could raise questions as they occur (on paper, in a question box, or in a designated space on the board), and there would be a period every week or so when the class would engage in a Socratic discussion around student-generated issues. It is a great developmental need of middle school students to be heard, to probe ideas, to sort out perspectives. A curriculum that has no time for these needs has no time for the human beings at the heart of the learning process. Pressures aside, few of us who teach and stay with teaching want to cast our votes in that direction.

8. Some of my students are very frustrated because "basic skills" always seem to slow them down and get in the way of their success. What can I do about that?

Many bright students who also have learning disabilities become very disenchanted with school. These students have minds that are active, inquisitive, and often quite creative. They grasp ideas quickly and generate wonderful plans, but they have difficulty reading or writing or sequencing ideas, and the combination is maddening. They are very aware of what they want to do and what it seems they should be able to do, but the doing never seems to work right.

It is very helpful for teachers of these students to spend a great deal of time emphasizing what the students *can* do rather than always focusing on what they *can't* do. If the student understands the concepts in the science chapter, have him storyboard them and make explanatory captions for the storyboards rather than requiring an essay, which will tie the student in knots and make him unable to share what he knows about science. If the student is required to write an essay in English, let her tape record her ideas and work from the recording to put the ideas on paper—or put each idea on a separate index card and then work with a peer or teacher to get them in order. We would not require a student in a wheelchair to run a sprint as the only way to demonstrate fitness. Rather, we'd work with that student to demonstrate strength in ways that make sense for the student's disability. The analogy holds for academics as well. That's not to say we shouldn't help the student work with important skills, but we should not work with "what's broken" until the student uses and stretches "what's fixed."

9. What should I do to help bright students from low-income families achieve?

The answer to this question depends upon the student, of course, but there are some important things to remember. Bright students from low-income households may lack many of the supports that we accept as givens with other bright students. Chances are, their parents care about them and their success as much as the parents of other students. However, their parents may not have been high performers in school and may not have the experience to "work the system" for their children in the same way parents of other bright kids do. There may not be as many books at home, no computer, and even markers and poster board may be in short supply. There may not be transportation to the library or anyone at home in the evening to oversee homework. These students may not have been in programs for students identified as gifted and, thus, may have missed the kinds of preparation for academic pursuits those programs instill. In the middle grades, bright students from these settings often struggle profoundly with peer pressure vs. academic pressure.

There is not a single right answer about how to help these students become excited about school and learning, but in general, the following "truths" prevail:

- Students need teachers to serve as mentors and coaches, not just as teachers.
- Students' attitudes about school may become more positive as they establish positive and enduring relationships with teachers who are willing to invest in them.
- Students are attracted to a curriculum that is engaging, curiosity-evoking, personally or culturally relevant, or otherwise "magnetic" for them.
- Students need adults who show them how to succeed and who are partners in their success.
- Students need a peer group that values achievement—even if the group is only two or three in number.
- Students need opportunities to see themselves in meaningful settings beyond school and home so that they have a sense of what it is they are aspiring to.
- Students need consistent, reassuring guidance during the middle school years regarding coursework, college entrance, scholarships, summer programs, and other gatekeepers to future success.
- Students need adults who can show them how to live successfully in two worlds—the one from which they come and the one to which they might go—and adults who can help them appreciate both.

Students who may lack some of the supports others have provide a great challenge and a real opportunity for teachers who want to make a positive difference in shaping young lives and are willing to invest what it takes to escort a young person into a positive future.

A Final Thought

The authors of this book are teachers in love with teaching and with middle school learners. For both of us, part of the joy of our work has been teaching—and being taught by—middle school students with high ability. After a combined tenure of more than 35 years in middle school classrooms, here is our summary guidance for other teachers who share a love of teaching and of young adolescents.

- **Remember that bright middle schoolers are young teens—and they need you in order to navigate adolescence successfully.**
- **Remember that bright middle schoolers will have rough spots and are entitled to them, just like all other growing human beings.**
- **Remember that they are learners—and that they need you to help extend their learning horizons.**
- **Remember that they need you to accept them and to find them worthwhile exactly as they are, just as they need your commitment to help them become something grander than they believe they could be.**
- **Remember to talk to them, listen to them, ask their opinions, study them.**
- **Remember to have grown-up conversations with them about science and current events, and novels—and to giggle with them about goofy things.**
- **Remember to help them be proud of their gifts—and humble in the face of the power of those gifts to make an impact on the world.**
- **Remember that as you stretch them, you will stretch as a teacher.**
- **And remember to enjoy the journey! ❖**